CATS AND YAMMERINGS
A Life Sketch in Verse

To

Ruth, Mema, and Beth

Parts of my life may be yours, in fact;
You know this better than I.
If these puny efforts seem lacking in tact,
Perhaps you'd be better to try.

(Suggested by R.W. Service's *Your Poem.)*

CATS AND YAMMERINGS

(Katzenyammerings)

A LIFE SKETCH IN VERSE

BY

ZACH M. ARNOLD

Pacific Grove, California

Distributed by:

The Boxwood Press
183 Ocean View Blvd.
Pacific Grove, CA 93950

Phone: 408—375-9110 * *Fax:* 408—375-0430

ISBN: 940168-30-8

Printed in USA

PREFACE

How often have you despaired of deciphering some unusual word or recondite allusion in a poem and given the whole thing up as a dead loss? Though there are relatively few such troublesome spots in the simple, unsophisticated verses of which I am capable, I thought it wise, at the risk of disgusting readers of superior intellect or experience and background, to include a glossary and some explanatory notes, to make the offerings more meaningful and palatable to those for whom the jargon or details from the author's own background and vintage might be unfamiliar.

A doggerel versifier at best (or worst), and certainly no poet, I delight in the sheer sound and rhythm of words, the hobby horse of a coronarily spavined septuagenarian. Jump onto the horse with me for a harmless little canter through some events in the life of one of God's simpler fools, who, though with both the heteronyms of *t-e-a-r-s* in his heart (i.e., the literal tears resulting from surgeon's knives and the metaphorical tears from weeping over the plight of much of the world's less fortunate human beings) yet has a song in his heart.

A word of perspective about section Five (The Banausic Side) of this work: a favorite former professor from my undergraduate days remarked, in a letter of congratulation on my belated attainment to full professorship, that my rise, though not meteoric, had been steady. You mustn't expect meteoric rises if you are happier on a lathe and milling machine than on academic senate committees. Banausic tendencies aren't, paradoxically enough, common in academe, nor are they particularly encouraged by the intellectual hierarchy. The banausiac's eloquent, though silent, protest against going through life with lily-white hands is viewed with surprise, suspicion and even contempt by the true intellectual and by the academic politician, but it seems a pity to go through life as a half person, missing the joys, delights, and satisfactions of Banausia, while taking care, of course, to avoid banausea, the malaise of banausic overindulgence.

The illustrations bearing a parenthetical (lower right) indication of their magnification are of miniature sculptural pieces made principally of polyethylene and polypropylene. They are intended merely to help set or suggest the tone of the accompanying poem. Some, particularly those accompanying blank and nonsense verse, are intentionally abstract or surrealistic, as would seem appropriate to the situation.

Zach M. Arnold

El Sobrante, Ca.
Spring, 1994

ACKNOWLEDGEMENTS

Ms. Mary E. Taylor has given helpful suggestions for improving the quality of many of the illustrations.

The cheerful professional guidance from Dr. Ralph Buchsbaum and all at Boxwood Press continues to make my path much easier and clearer.

From World War II days, my laboratory sergeant, Lewis G. Wells, and my commanding officer, Colonel Frank E. Stinchfield, did much on numerous occasions to make my army lot a happy one, and on one especially memorable occasion General Paul Hawley, Chief Surgeon of the European Theater of Operations, was particularly generous to a lowly T/5 whom he commended for his orderly services when he should have court-martialled him for scorching his pinks in a sleepy-eyed, wee-hours-of-the-morning ironing orgy.

My wife, Jean, tolerant, understanding, forgiving, and always helpful, has done much to make the fifty years of my adult life as happy as my parents and three sisters did the earlier ones.

Lastly, our four feline waifs have patiently, albeit unwittingly, served as models, thus fostering my jejune efforts at ailurophilous artistry, and their propensity for sitting on papers —especially on valuable ones—whenever such are carelessly left lying about has taught me foresight in caring for finished drawings or camera-ready copy destined for the publisher.

Zach M. Arnold

CONTENTS

PART TWO
ARMY

PART THREE
CHILDHOOD

PART FOUR
MUSIC

PART FIVE
THE BANAUSIC SIDE

PART SIX
A MUSING GRACE

PROLOGUE

Cats and yammerings about warriors bold,
This and much more we'll here unfold.
No murder or mayhem, it's all pretty tame,
But it's all true stuff about life's game.

Some of the problems we all have to face,
As we try to be happy and avoid disgrace,
Are dealt with at length. But, oddly enough,
Most of the poems are light-hearted stuff,

For Fate has dealt lightly and kindly with me.
I'm now growing old and content to be:
Happier, in fact, to work without pay;
Busily challenged by ev'ry new day.

But that's the secret I've just disclosed
Of one who is now quite happily disposed
Toward life and the process of growing old:
A cheerier fate than we often are told.

Oct. 17, 1993

Blank verse we need upon the *verso* blank,
At least it's needed for a lively pun.
It makes a type of oxymoron, too.
We'll take in turn each *verso* blank and try
To use blank verse to maculate the page.
The sense is of no consequence, it's just
To have it there to see and try to know
The noble role it has to play and why:
Deoxygenate an oxymoron and then
Let's elate on the residue moronic
Of our paronomasic delinquency.

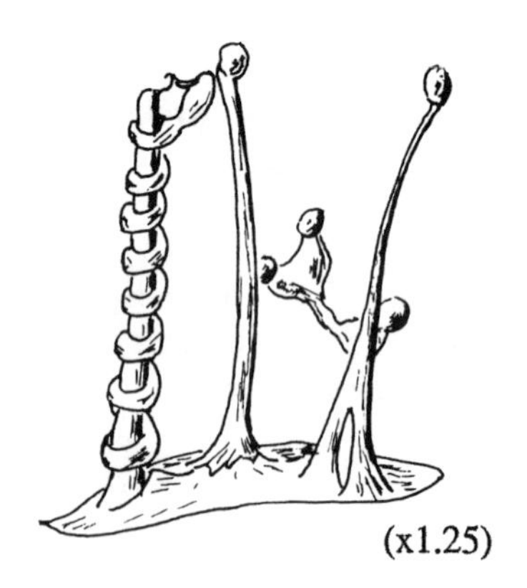

(x1.25)

PART ONE

CATS

Let's now inflame an *ignis fatuus*
To see the thrust of sheer nihility
Against *simplex mundities* prostrate.
(Something Horace would appreciate.)
If nullibicity alone remains,
We'll keep it nomothetic and jejune.
Why leave a page like this immaculate,
When maculae abound on ev'ry side,
Though not a jot of thought-provoking tittle
Accrues to elevate the lowly tone?

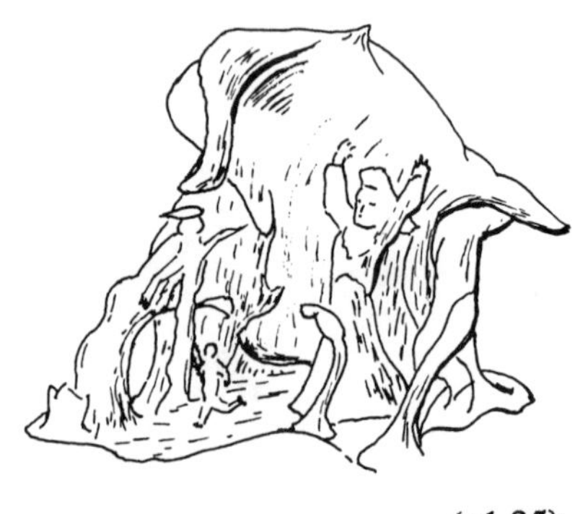

(x1.25)

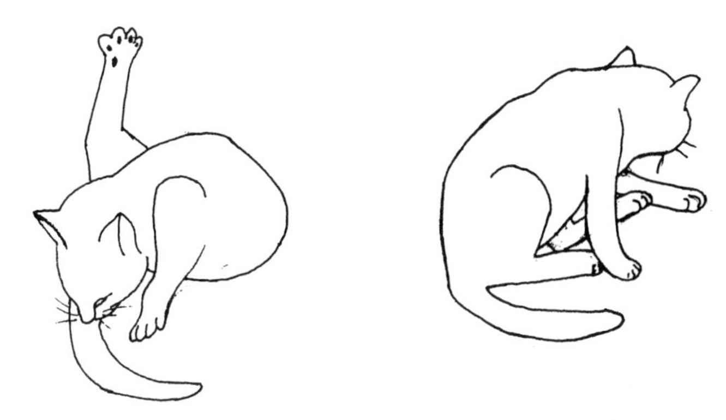

ABLUTIONS AND CONTORTIONS

Do you know any humans who cats can match in the matter of daily ablutions,
Or any who the contortions of cats can match with such clever solutions?
Contortionists, yes, do remarkable feats, but never do they these combine
With balneal graces blended in to enhance the aesthetic design.

If ever you've taken the time with a watch to see just how long it takes
For a long-haired tom to scrub himself down as his post-prandial toilet he makes,
I think you'll agree that few can compare, in matters balneatory,
With just such a cat after a meal in all his ablutional glory.

The bones of a cat—or at least the joints—seem to be made of rubber;
Whichever way they wish them to bend, they seem undeterred by demurrer.
Perhaps this explains why their limbs they can thrust and twist through angles absurd,
So in balneotherapeutics their achievement's the very last word.

Lavational gymnastics are delightful to watch; our cats put on quite a show:
One leg goes up, but which one will follow is just not so easy to know.
As the bathing proceeds, a posture upright gives way to one in repose,
And when it's all done, the cat coils around for his post-ablutional doze.

I find it relaxing to just sit and watch those feline contortions abstersive;
I also find it helps me to write in a manner that's far more discursive.
Whoever dreamt that the lingual abstergence in ordinary feline ablutions
Could foster linguistic abstergence in achieving prosodic solutions?

Jan. 29, 1994

ADDICTIONS

Some are addicted to drugs or drink, some to lung-rotting smoke,
But, please, don't laugh when I tell you of ours; most surely it isn't a joke.
It all came about some years ago through a quirk of circumstance,
And I confess we seem mesmerized, behaving as though in a trance.

Our will no longer dictates to us, superceded it's been, eclipsed
By a force that leaves all our plans in shreds, all our intentions outstrips.
However strong and willful our hopes and adamant may be our views,
We're led by the power of our latest addiction along paths that we didn't choose.

We start off our day with a pattern laid out, a schedule quite rigid and sound,
But hardly do we leave our nice warm beds before a new course we've found.
We didn't choose it—Heaven forbid !—Oh, no, on us it was thrust.
If I tell you about it in all its detail, I think you'll agree 'twas unjust.

We never were able to don proper clothes before the demands began;
Not strident nor rude, but insistent they were, causing a change in our plan.
Before we could feed, four pairs of eyes, gazing with a trust quite sublime,
Began their plea for a morning meal, knowing that now was the time.

So we fed them all well, their four-course meal: meat, kibbles, milk and cheeze.
Just the type of food they desired, finicky tastes sure to please.
Once they were fed, then we could dine, on oatmeal and a bit of dry toast.
Somehow I feel they came out the best; I know that they got the most.

So this is the course our addiction now takes: the needs of our cats come first.
But of all the addictions that we might have had, I doubt that this is the worst.
This one we've had for only three years, but we're hoping for quite a few more;
To us considerable pleasure they've given, our furry felines four.

Jan. 29, 1994

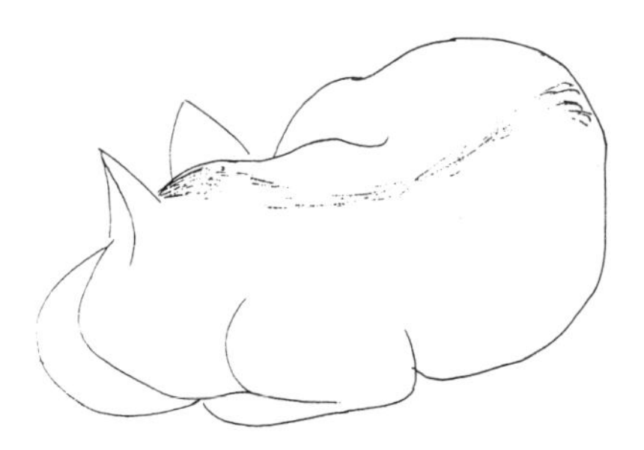

THE AFTERNOON NAP

Five out of six take an afternoon nap,
And if we miss it we raise quite a flap.
Chummy and I go to our beds
And cover all up, even our heads.

A drawer of my desk is pulled out for her,
Her wee woolen blanket is spotted with fur.
On warm sunny days Ces can be found
Asleep in a nest of leaves on the ground.

Wedgie prefers the roof where its flat,
An ideal spot for a somnolent cat.
The roof of my shop is for Mom's siesta,
Secure in a spot where none can molest her.

Jean alone of the six stays awake;
Never a moment's repose does she take
'Til darkness descends, her day's work is done:
She then goes to rest with the sun.

Oh, what a comfort to sleep after lunch,
The four cats and I, but not in a bunch!
After their nap the cats are content
To just lie about, their energies spent.

It's food they require to start off anew,
And after their meal they know what to do:
They clean themselves well and have a short play
Before settling down to sleep 'til next day.

Feb. 2, 1993

AILUROPOESY

Ailuropoesy is not for all;
For some it lacks appeal.
When I succcumbed I can't recall,
But my love for it I can't conceal.

Poems and cats just seem to blend;
Both have charm and grace.
Each moves along from end to end
With ease, what'er the pace.

The challenge to me is just as great
To understand good verse
As the ways of cats to appreciate,
And accept for better or for worse.

Now, when the two of them you blend
Through thought and love sincere,
Some joy, perhaps, it may portend
To ease our sojourn here.

Will the one who writes or the one who reads
Benefit the most from the chore?
No matter which; if it meets one's needs
Why should we ask for more?

Jan 7, 1993

APPEARANCE

Meticulous care, conscientious concern are attributes normal for cats;
Rubbing and scrubbing to keep themselves clean, they are not content with mere pats.
Washing and preening with moistened forearm for spots that are difficult to reach
Are some of the skills and tricks of the trade their mother takes great pains to teach.

Contortions unique and attitudes rare they assume in the course of the task;
To be left alone to get on with the job, as a rule, is just all that they ask.
You may stand and look on, but don't interfere, they're completely absorbed in the chore;
If you pat them or stroke them before they are done, they just start the licking once more.

The whole of their body, with vigour that's fierce, their tongue with its rasp-like expanse
Subjects to a licking that's lovely to watch, their natural charm to enhance.
And when they are done, all tidy and clean, they now need restorative sleep.
If the weather is cold, they coil in a ball and drop off in slumber quite deep.

Personal pride and hygiene come first, no matter how busy their day;
Appearance and health, top-ranking concerns: other cares to these give way.
Eating and sleeping are essential, of course, and are affairs they take to their heart,
But it all seems to go to a praiseworthy end: appearance, both healthy and smart.

Jan. 23, 1993

AWAKE WITH THE CATS

They're in at five, before it's dark,
And want their evening meal.
The fact that they have lost their spark
No more do they conceal.

After that it's wash and clean
And settle for the night.
All bedded down and covered up,
Completely lost from sight.

They slumber on and have their dreams,
And seldom stir at all;
To see them there it surely seems
They'll stay until we call.

But this is not to be...

At four A.M. they rise again,
One wakes the others up.
They wash once more, and then its plain
It's time to have a sup.

They eat again, and then it's time
To start the day anew.
So out they go in bliss sublime,
And leave the house to stew.

And stew we do, we're all awake,
But what a chance it gives
To use the time and with it make
A poem that really lives!

And so, from turn of circumstance
Some good can come our way:
We only have to use the chance
Of turning night to day.

Dec. 27, 1992

CATS' RIGHTS

The cats now are eating, with tails in repose;
They lay them right out, straight on the floor.
A plate is put down, just under each nose,
A convenient arrangement, but no room for more.

They fill up the kitchen at mealtimes, you see.
With dishes and bodies and tails all stretched out,
They leave little room for Jeanie and me
For preparing our supper and moving about.

But life with four cats will ever be thus;
You must re-arrange your affairs.
And if you don't want all the bother and fuss,
You'll have to abridge the rights that are theirs,

For they will not change as easily as you.
Standards they have that are dear.
So whatever they wish, whatever they do,
You must conform; your role is quite clear.

Jan. 2, 1993

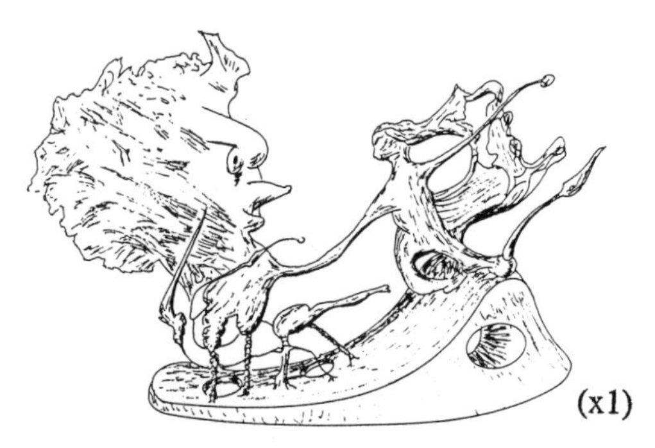
(x1)

CES AND THE CHRISTMAS STUFF

Their favorite aunt, who lives in Maine,
Had sent the gifts by aeroplane.
Three thousand miles to us they flew,
The contents only the dear aunt knew.

Three little packages, neatly wrapped
And tied with ribbons red,
Each with a greeting capped,
And this is what it said:

"To the Arnold felines from your Aunt in Maine
Who hopes ere long to see you again."
This set the stage for a chain of events
That soon were to have dire consequence.

Ces was the first to find a gift;
He eyed it well, then stooped and sniffed.
One big sniff was quite enough
To let him know he'd got THE STUFF.

He grabbed at the parcel and began to tear
At ribbons and papers and all that was there,
'Til the wrapping came off and he could see in,
And this is the point where the fun did begin.

If you've ever seen a druggy, wild from his pills,
Or a true alcoholic soused to the gills,
You'll have an idea of the magic spell
Cast on the cat by that parcel's smell.

A little sachet, a bouquet of string,
And poor Ces became a maniacal thing.
Some pinches of catnip were all it contained,
But Ces's contortions could not be restrained.

He tumbled and tossed and he tore at the bag
'Til he ripped it apart and left it a rag.
Some small bits of catnip scattered around,
Some string and some cotton, all that was found.

The frenzy that tormented poor little Ces
Had us both worried, we frankly confess,
For we'd never before seen this well-mannered cat,
Self-control lost, behaving like that.

But what of the response to their bags by the others?
Wedgie's was boredom, unlike his wee mother's,
Who looked with suspicion, responded with flight,
While Chummy immediately started to fight.

The fight that she waged was vigorous enough,
But in comparison with Ces's was not very tough,
Which just goes to show the response in such scenes
May well be detemined by the mix of one's genes.

Dec. 25, 1992

CES LIKES BACH

Ces is our gentle long-haired male,
And this poem, I fear, is a long-haired tale
Of his love for music of the heavier type
And his utter disdain for musical tripe.

My practice begins with some light-hearted stuff,
But we both of this soon have enough.
At this stage Ces has just entered the room,
His post-prandial chore himself now to groom.

The music goes on, the cleaning does, too,
Each occupied with the task he must do.
Brahms and Chopin, followed by Liszt;
Ces is now cleaning the places he'd missed.

With fingers now nimble, it's time for some Bach,
While Ces of his cleaning begins to take stock.
Partitas and fugues and two-part inventions,
Now Ces can reveal his own true intentions.

I just have achieved an adequate stride,
When Ces toddles over and sits at my side.
Of all the obstacles to playing the piano,
The one I prefer is a cat at my elbow.

Not for long content to stay
Just at my side as I try to play,
He soon moves over onto my lap
And settles down to take a nap.

And so, at last, we've reached the end
Of the long-haired tale of my furry friend
Who finds Bach's music so terrific
The effect on him is quite soporific.

Sept. 18, 1993

CHUMMY AND THE RAIN

Chummy likes to watch the rain,
Just like we, as kids, would do.
To watch the drops race down the pane,
A game not there when skies are blue.

Or in her box outside the door,
Hypnotized by the shimmering stream,
The glistening rivulets on the floor
Carry her away in a blissful dream.

Where does she go when she drifts away?
To a magic land where dreams come true,
Where cats can eat and sleep all day
With never an irksome task to do.

Where cars and dogs can pose no threat,
Unpleasant noise and sound are banned;
They never need go to see the vet,
All is arranged as they have planned.

Perhaps they dream of a magic land,
Some feline Shangrila,
Where all is bright and grand,
No matter who you are.

Until the dawn of that blissful day
When ours perfection find,
We strive in our own imperfect way
To give them peace of mind.

Jan. 14, 1993

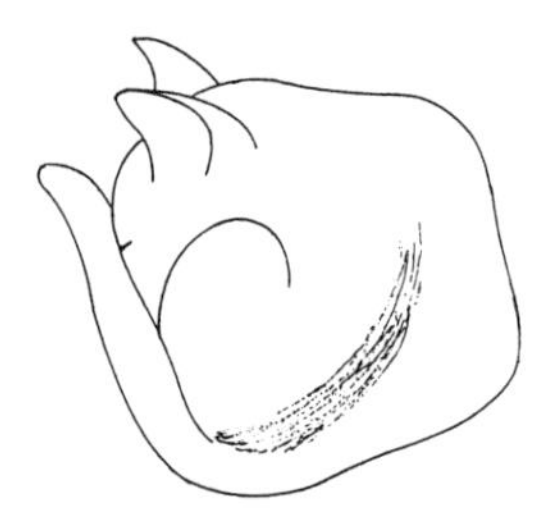

CHUMMY'S ROUTINE

There's nothing haphazard about her affairs, the pattern she sets is so clear;
Digressions from this are simply not made; to her her routine is quite dear.
She likes to go out and start off her day before all the birds are awake,
For that way it's easy to sneak up on one and of it her breakfast to make.

After a meal and a bit of a romp, she's ready to come for a nap;
For an hour or two while the sun warms up, a bed is preferred to a lap.
Then she likes to go out once again and scamper around in the yard,
Though to entice her two brothers at this time of day is often uncommonly hard.

She often comes in for a wee bit of lunch, then to her window upstairs
To watch the young dog in the garden next door as he 'round with his teddy-bear tears.
Before very long, fatigue takes its toll, she soon settle down on my bed
And waits to be covered with her own little blanket, covered right up, from tail to head.

By mid afternoon she's up and about, with her brothers out romping again.
They tear through the garden, up and down trees, content in their lovely domain
'Til hunger o'ercomes them just after dark and they gather for their evening repast,
Brought to the lawn on their own special tray, whence all is demolished quite fast.

They start off with kibbles, canned meat of their choice, all with warm milk washed down,
And topped off with cheese diced to small cubes, though Wedgie on this seems to frown.
Mom always comes to eat with her kids, happy to eat what they leave;
All four then settle to clean themselves up with a diligence hard to believe.

While I play the piano for an hour or so, they scamper about outside.
Chummy is then ready to come in to bed, the others have places to hide.
But first she must dash up and down stairs and then jump into the tub
And lie there stretched out, waiting for me to give her her nocturnal rub.

Then to the window right by my bed to watch all the lights she can see;
But soon she starts blinking and tottering a bit, now she's as sleepy as can be.
So it's onto my bed to get covered up, her slumbers now deep there to start.
I lie there and read for an hour or two, but then from my buddy must part.

For the time has now come to scoop up my pal and take her to Mummy next door,
Where she soon cuddles up in nocturnal bliss with a purr and occasional snore.
And so the night passes, the two of them there are perfectly matched in their sleep;
Chummy's content and her day is complete if to her routine we but keep.

Mar. 21, 1993

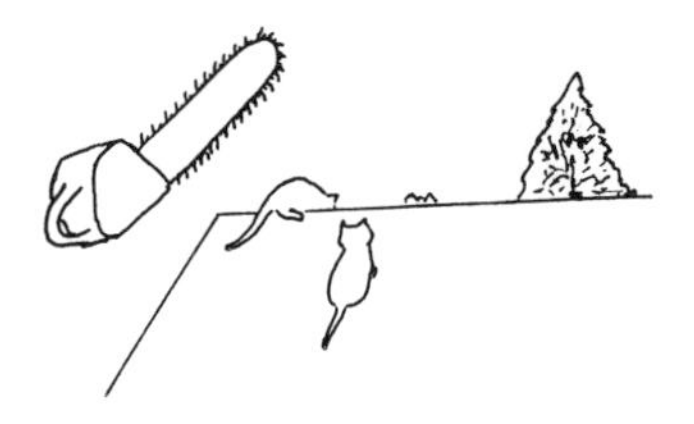

THE DAY THE TREE SURGEON CAME

The roof of our house is the cat's domain; they think it was built for them.
It's varied enough for every need, it satisfies everyone's whim:
The flat part is great for lying stretched out and soaking up lots of sun;
The pitched parts are exciting, a challenge, a wonderful place to have fun.

Mum is content, as a rule, to just sit and watch her three kids at play:
Now they are grown and bigger than she, she wisely keeps out of their way.
But the three kids all know and respect their dear Mum and try to be gentle with her,
While she on her part is still their Mum and is often seen licking their fur.

The dance I must do to avoid the cats on the roof with its pitch so high,
At three score and ten is a sight to see, a treat that none will deny.
One of the cats always must come to join the leaves in my bag,
Which entices the others to join in the fun, the three of them then playing tag.

The leaves, of course, are tipped out, the task must be started anew,
But the pitch of the roof and the danger entailed makes it not easy to do.
The wise thing for me is to clean off the roof when the cats are elsewhere engaged.
Without any cats you'll have peace and quiet; your patience will not be outraged.

A fine way to clear the roof of all cats is to have the tree surgeon come.
The four disappear like snow from a dike at the monstrous chain-saw hum.
But the sawdust that's left all over the roof when the limbs are well pruned away
Is a great deal more work and not nearly the fun of three little cats at play.

So, if I had my choice 'twixt chain-saw and cats, there's no doubt where my vote would lie:
The three balls of fur for playmates I'd choose, to the pattern they set I'd comply.
The saw is atrocious, its din is abhorent, there's nought to commend it but speed;
Though rooftops are frightful, with cats they're delightful, meeting one's uppermost need.

Mar. 11, 1993

EDGY WEDGIE

Wedgie's quite edgy, we wish it weren't so,
But he's been that way from the start.
Wherever his Mum went, there he would go,
It was she, not he, who was smart.

He was always bewildered from the day he was born;
He just could not cope with life's ills.
As a kitten he often would just sit forlorn,
While the others partook of its thrills.

Now that he's grown, he's still not at ease;
His favorite haunt is under a chair.
And there he remains, ignoring our pleas;
We just have to leave him there.

When we have guests, he tears out of doors
And may even rush headlong into rain.
Any kind of excitement he simply abhors
And takes to his heels once again.

Chummy, his sister, had much rather be
Right in the middle of things.
All that happens she's eager to see,
Eager to know what each day brings.

Some of us humans are much like poor Wedgie;
Life's too exciting to take it all in.
The hustle and bustle makes us all edgy,
Overwhelmed by perpetual din.

From life's daily rigours we need our release,
From noise and strife we gladly defect.
Like Wedgie, we require a great deal of peace,
A chance to dream and reflect.

Jan. 17, 1993

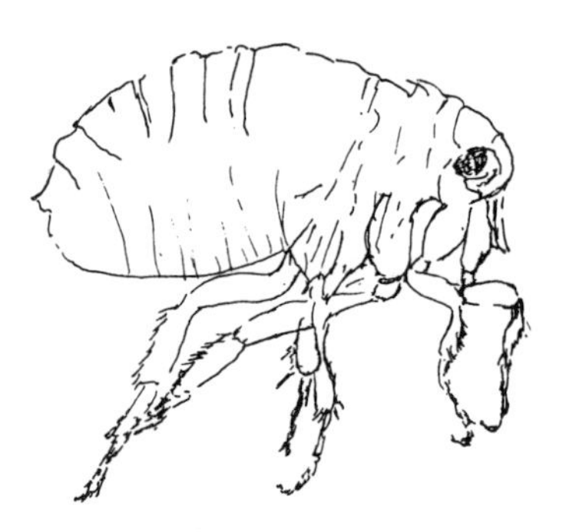

FLEAS

PLEASE, LEND YOUR LITTLE EARS TO MY FLEAS
FLEAS, LEND YOUR LITTLE EARS TO MY PLEAS *

Doesn't your bed have fleas? Ah, you don't know what you're missing,
Though some of the things they do, I fear, may not be just what you're wishing!
If you haven't experienced the ecstasy of sharing your bed with a flea,
I fear you haven't known the fun a truly eventful night can be.

Some folks seem ashamed to admit that in their bed are fleas;
The mere idea of having them there creates a deadly unease,
But, if you with cats have a friendly rapport and admit them into your life,
You'll also have to find a place for the fleas with which they are rife.

When I was a child the best friends I had were animals in great variety:
Cats and cows, chickens and calves, I always enjoyed their society.
The next fifty years were too busy for pets, we hadn't the time to spare,
But now the declining years of our lives we've decided with cats we shall share.

Or, at least, the cats decided for us: a mom and her kittens three
Adopted our yard and entered our lives as happily as they could be.
Now they've become an integral part of our daily and nightly routine,
We've adapted quite well to a role about which at first we just were not keen.

The sincerest form of flattery I've known is to have one of our cats decide
That he'd like to spend a part of the night snuggled abed at my side.
Of course, by one or two o'clock he needs to have a wee snack,
And after the meal he wants to go out, I'm reluctant to invite him back.

Now, you might think that that is the end of the nocturnal saga I've told,
As the principal character in the charade departs in the night so bold,
But, sad to relate, there's more yet to come, there's a sequel we mustn't forget;
The events of the night are still crowding in, you've simply not heard the full story yet.

About the time you get back to sleep, you're awakened by a curious sensation:
Something is crawling about on your back too small for direct confrontation.
With a vigor ferocious you scratch where it itches, but all, I fear, that seems to do
Is shift the commotion to somewhere else, where it all commences anew.

By this time you are fully awake and will be for an hour or two,
A good time to rise from the nice warm bed that your writhings have left all askew
And spread back the sheets to prowl for the pest that's disrupted your slumber so sound,
Knowing full well you'll never relax until the wee culprit you've found.

The best tool I've found for killing a flea is a six-inch file from my shop;
It is far more effective than fingers and nails in thwarting the flea and his hop.
When you've managed to smear a half dozen or so flea carcasses out on the sheets,
You'll find the accomplishment effective indeed insomnia soon to defeat.

Most of life's problems are too tough for me, with them I can't seem to cope,
But for dealing with fleas I have a technique; with it I do have some hope:
Pull back the sheets before going to bed and conduct a careful inspection;
Then with your file annihilate them all, the victims of ruthless detection!

May 6, 1993

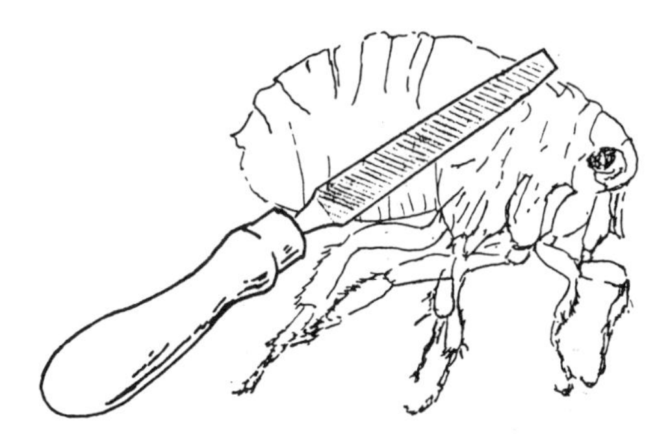

*A play on the song title *Please, Lend your Little Ears to My Pleas.*

THE FLY SAFARI

Hold your breath and calm your fears and, please, try not to worry,
Though adventure high is in the air and the house is all in a flurry,
A day to remember above all others, for Grandpa and Chummy are out on safari.
A secret they share but will not divulge: a great juicy fly is their innocent quarry.

Chummy just adores the chance to hunt and chase about for flies,
But very seldom catches one, no matter how hard she tries.
Then Grandpa she saw swatting at flies and doing it with lots of success.
A nice little pile of flies he soon made; she eagerly gobbled the mess.

The next time he the swatter fetched Chummy was really prepared:
She danced about and miaowed and miaowed, her teeth and claws were all bared.
He would swat and she would pounce to eat each one he would stun,
And soon between the two of them the deadly chore was done.

Now whenever Grandpa goes to get the lethal swatter,
Chummy starts to fume and sweat, her passions all get hotter.
The chase for her is all the rage, with tasty morsels, too.
She's got Grandpa trained quite well his job for her to do.

Now whenever the unholy pair set out to hunt for flies,
You know Grandpa will try to swat the ones wee Chummy spies.
But if he sees one before she does and brings it crashing down,
You know that she on the juicy bite will not be one to frown.

And so for Cummy a fly safari is a source of endless joy:
The thrill of the chase and the meal of flies never seem to cloy.
The fly community is well advised to keep a low profile
When this deadly duo decide to launch their vicious hunts so vile.

Mar. 8, 1993

THE GENTLE CAT WITH THE DROOPING TAIL

His name is really Wedgewood, but we seldom call him that;
It's often changed to Reggie, he's such a gentle cat!
But then again it's Wedgie, he answers just the same;
He even comes a runnin' when Reginal is the name.

Tail held high with pride, his pace a gentle trot,
He's nearly alway first at meals to see what food they've got.
A hearty trencherman, with a healthy appetite,
His custom is to eat his fill, he does so with delight.

One day he turned up missing from the usual prandial flap;
Both high and low we searched for him; at last we found the chap.
We picked him up and brought him in to feed without the troop;
'Twas then we noticed with chagrin the piteous tail adroop.

No more held high, aloft and proud, a healthy sight to see,
But sagging down, a sight so sad, and held most tenderly.
A lump there was, swelled with pain, poor chap could hardly stand;
He wouldn't let us look at it or touch it with our hand.

We put him in a sunny spot, one safe, with lots to eat,
And let him sleep and eat all day, alone in his retreat.
That day and then the next and next he mostly lay around,
He made no haste to join the group, just lay there on the ground.

But then one day he struggled out to join the other three,
His tail was now half mast, a hopeful sight to see.
Next day the tail was nearly up, the pain had left the lump,
And then at last it came erect and he could run and jump.

How gentle through it all was he, a calmness so sublime,
He simply laid his body down to give it healing time.
When all was right again, he surely didn't fail
To show his gratitude and raise that lovely tail.

Dec. 20, 1992

THE GOURMET TREAT

Chicken livers and oatmeal, a favorite mealtime treat;
It takes some preparation, it's not just heat and eat.
A pound of livers: freeze 'em hard to simplify the slicing,
Then change the slices into cubes by very careful dicing.

Boil this all in a pot of water to turn the blood to grey,
Then add oatmeal, while stirring still, and let it boil away
'Til all the flakes are blended in to form a mushy mess
That for the cats is soon to be a source of happiness.

Before it cools, without a doubt, the aroma will have spread
And rounded up the hungry cats, now clamouring to be fed.
A seething mass, a milling mob, is gathered at the door,
And though they look a dozen strong, they're really only four.

Four cats; four plates piled high with this their noon repast;
You'd be amazed, indeed, to see how short it lasts.
But what a joy to stand and watch this happy mealtime scene:
Four cats replete, with bulging tums, four dishes licked quite clean!

Dec. 22, 1992

THE GRACIE TRILOGY

I

GRACIE, THE CALICO MANX

Someone must have dumped wee Gracie in our neighborhood.
She went from house to house to find exactly where she stood.
One house after another refused to take her in;
The pickings as she started out must have seemed quite thin.

But then she came to us, and what a tale she told
As she stood atop my workshop roof her problems to unfold.
Rebuffs she'd had, that was clear; she told about them all.
A sadder tale than hers, I fear, I simply can't recall.

I told her that we had four cats and hadn't room for more.
As I turned away and walked inside, she followed to the door
And stood there pleading so, with a heart so filled with pain,
I had to yield and let her in; I couldn't stand the strain.

All the time that this went on an endless stream of woes
Told what a life she'd led, an endless stream of foes.
I opened up a tin of meat, diced her up some cheese,
Gave her a nice warm bowl of milk, my answer to her pleas.

She, of course, thought this was great, she'd found a home at last!
This was the sort of place she'd sought, she'd now adopt us fast.
She truffed right in to a hearty meal, polished off the lot,
And asked if she could look around to see the home she'd got.

She wandered through the house and yard, inspecting ev'ry nook,
And came to say she liked it all, especially the cook.
She'd come to us bereft of names, to find one was our chore;
"Gracie" seemed to fit the bill, and so we sought no more.

The problem now arose, of course, of what to tell our four,
And see if they were all prepared to have us take one more.
The boys and Mum seemed quite at ease, but Chummy was in a huff:
She thought that she and the other three were really quite enough.

So we asked our neighbor next door, a gentle chap and kind,
If he would take wee Gracie: he said he wouldn't mind.
And that is how we came to have a calico Manx next door
Who feels it right, after eating at home, to come to us for more.

Oct. 14, 1993

II

WHEN GRACIE NEEDS A DRINK

When Gracie comes to visit us, we know just what comes first:
She rushes to the bathroom, there to quench her thirst.
She much prefers a plastic bowl in the basin there upstairs,
But after that she wastes no time in cleaning up her hairs.

The plastic bowl's her very own, she uses it with pride,
But to help her drink with ease, we turn it on its side.
If this sometimes we fail to do, with a paw she gives a little push
To show she needs our help—no beating 'round the bush.

Though Gracie's just a guest with us, she treats our house like home;
The dishes we keep for our own cats she uses as her own.
Of course, she'd had a hearty meal before she came to us,
But it's easy to devour another without a lot of fuss.

There's surely no denying we've a soft spot in our heart
For that wee calico Manx from whom we'd hate to part.
As she sits there in our kitchen and laps up nice warm milk,
We'll surely keep succumbing to Gracie and her ilk.

We feel that we are lucky to have such guests as she,
Who likes to come and visit whenever she is free.
Her lapping up warm milk brightens up our day,
And then we know she's eager to get outside and play.

Gracie is a latch-key cat, she needs some neighbor friends,
And this is how we feel, indeed, that we can make amends,
Let the little creature know the folks next door do care
Both day and night—no matter when—if her own folks are not there.

Oct. 13, 1993

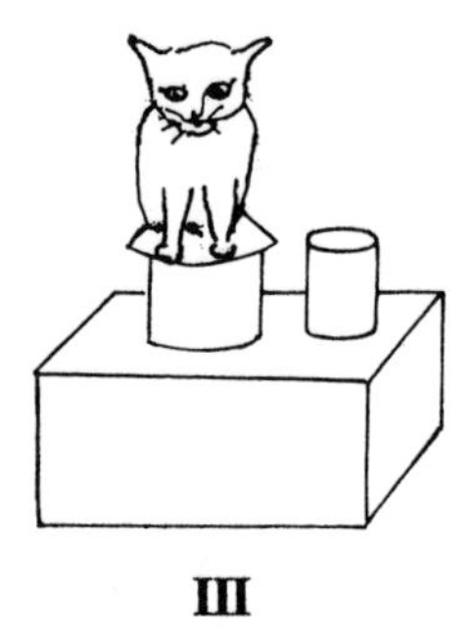

III

THE RIVALS

Gracie on the chimney pot,
Chummy on the prowl;
Any love they might have got
Emerges as a growl.

They've never been at ease, those two,
Since Gracie moved next door.
We simply know not what to do
To give them peace once more.

Gracie loves to come to us and have an extra meal,
But such an act of kindliness to Chum does not appeal.
She lies in wait for the stub-tail Manx
Determined to stop her neighborly pranks.

But still brave Gracie comes on up;
She skirts each ambush set,
For when she knows its time to sup,
She doesn't sit and fret.

Our stubby-tail friend, the calico Manx,
Has the appetite of two;
She eats and runs, with little thanks,
She hardly stops to chew.

And then outside she waits for Jean
To see her down the street,
In case she be by Chummy seen,
Protection should they meet.

Then came the day that Gracie left;
Her family moved away,
Which left our Chummy quite bereft:
She really rues the day.

And now she sits at her window pane,
Wondering where Gracie went.
If only her rival would come back again,
Wee Chummy would be content.

But this, I fear, is not to be.

Dec. 31, 1992

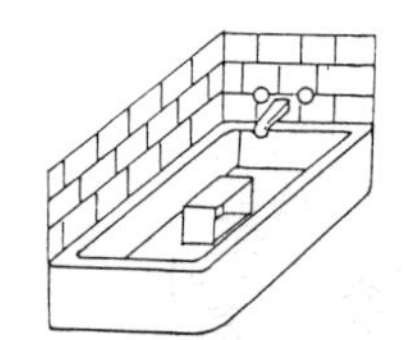

A HOME FOR CHUMMY

The gang's arrived, the time is nigh to feed the little lot;
Let's just pop out and see right now the lovely group we've got.
There's Mum and Chum and Wedge, then Ses, who's always late;
Each one likes a special place and each a special plate.

For Mum it's best up near the lawn, so she can run and hide,
And Wedge is always sure to be close there by her side.
He's proud to be her champion bold, for big and strong is he;
He crouches there 'til she's replete, he's twice as large as she.

Now Chum prefers her meal to be apart from the common herd;
The spot she wants might seem at first to be a bit absurd,
For up she trots and has her meal in the empty bathroom tub;
But this is really not so odd: she slept there as a cub.

And this is how it happened:

One evening mild, by the setting sun, Mum and her kittens three
Were playing 'round the kitchen door as happy as could be.
Then all at once Mum took fright, ran off and called her lot;
The boys ran off right after her, but Chummy must have not.

She ran instead into the shop and hid behind some shelves;
She lay there unbeknownst to Mum and even to ourselves.
All night she stayed, alone and cold: no food, no warmth, no company.
Next day I heard a little meiow, a pitiful sight to see:

A trembling three-inch ball of fur, terrified with fright,
Cold and hungry, lonesome, too, what an awful night!
We picked her up and warmed her well, all snuggled in my coat,
Then nice warm milk, fed drop by drop, went down her little throat.

Into the tub: a cardboard box turned upon its side,
A hotwater bottle, wrapped in a towel, a good warm place to hide.
So that is how a home was found for poor wee baffled Chum,
And this is how she came to be estranged from little Mum.

Dec. 22, 1992

MUM INVARIABLY STEPS ASIDE

Mum invariably steps aside
To let her children feed,
A part of her maternal pride
And total lack of greed.

When first with tiny kittens three,
As she lay there on her side,
'Twas foreordained ever thus to be:
She'd always step aside.

So when the three were quite grown up
And twice as large as she,
When'er the line was formed to sup,
Way at the rear she'd always be.

How noble is such sacrifice,
How honorable is her breed!
She steps aside, not once or twice,
But ev'ry time there's need.

How nice 'twould be if now and then
The kids would let their Mum come first,
Just step aside and let her in
To eat her fill and quench her thirst.

But we are there to fill a need,
When all is done and said:
To see, in spite of children's greed,
That Mum goes not unfed.

And feed she does, we see to that;
She gets a special treat,
And though she's quite a little cat,
She sups until replete.

The least that we can do for her
Is give her lots to eat.
And this we do without demur,
It's such a simple feat.

Jan. 2, 1993

(x1)

MUMMY AND CHUMMY ALL NIGHT LONG

Mummy and Chummy all night long in restful slumber lie;
To find two pals more closely knit, you really mustn't try.
They've worked it out, there's space for both there on the little bed,
A special blanket's pulled right up to cover Chummy's head.

Chum starts out coiled in a ball to build up needed heat,
But when her body's nice and warm, out stretch all four feet.
Two reach to Mummy's face as though they need to know
That she'll be there what'er befalls, to ward off any foe.

The other two stretch down full length along their guardian's side.
Unlike the nights out in the wild, there's here no need to hide.
From time to time faint groans and squeaks emerge from little Chum;
Perhaps a dream, perhaps a flea, or maybe gas within the tum.

To calm the fears, Mom reaches down and girds the sleeping mass,
Her soothing arm, all soft and warm, soon helps the worries pass.
How wondrous are the nights thus spent by such a disparate pair,
The fears allayed of a creature wild to know a human's there.

Dec. 21, 1992

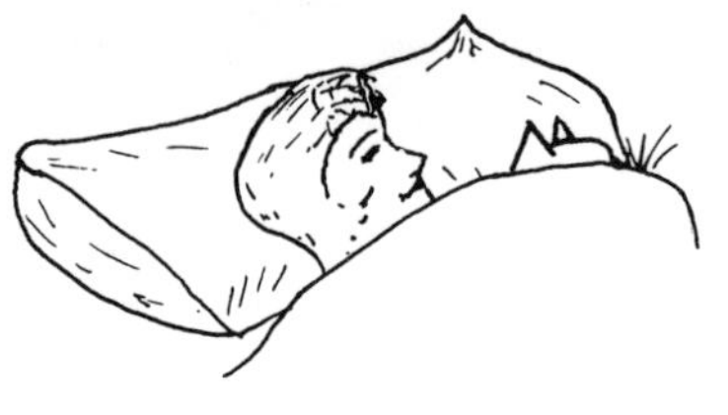

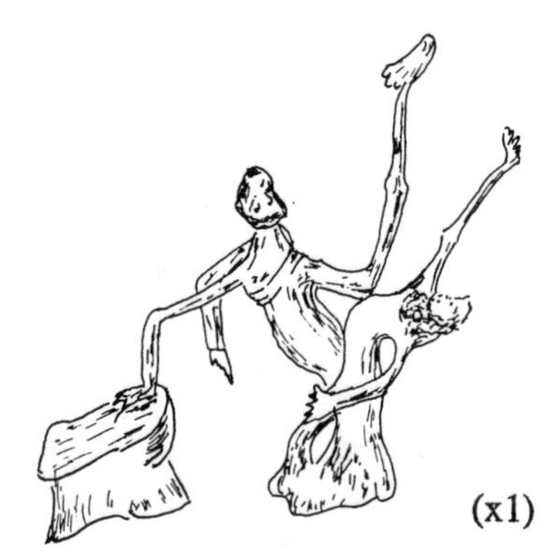

NOW WE CAN SLEEP

We can't retire for the night 'til we know
The cats are all comfy and warm,
'Til they are all fed and tucked in just so,
Knowing they'll come to no harm.

Chummy's in first, she's ready by five,
And starts out the night on my bed.
To see her you'd think that she's barely alive,
Covered right up, including her head.

Wedgie's inside on his own special chair,
It's green and his own little blanket is too.
Right after supper to him it seems fair
His own preparations for slumber to do.

Ces washes and cleans for a half hour or so;
His long fur is tricky indeed,
But then with his Afghan to sleep he will go:
Bed is for him a real need.

Though she won't come inside, we know Mum's okay
In her wee well-lined basin, her joy and her pride.
We know that she's happy right there to stay:
She's warm and she's dry, with food at her side.

Now we can sleep, our own minds at rest,
With four cosy cats, all safe and secure.
Each has selected the spot that suits best.
When they are sleeping they look so demure.

You'd think that like this all would be well,
The night and our sleep would be long.
The truth, I'm afraid, is less pleasant to tell:
Our anticipations were wrong.

Half through the night at least one of the three
That sleep in the house needs food.
This wakes the other two and Jean and me
To come down and see to the brood.

But once they are fed they seem quite content
To settle back down or just go outside,
While we return to sleep as we meant,
Trying frustration to hide.

And so go our nights, awake and asleep,
The cats by it seem undismayed.
Our sleep—when we get it—is ever so deep,
Though disruption's the price that we've paid.

Jan.18, 1993

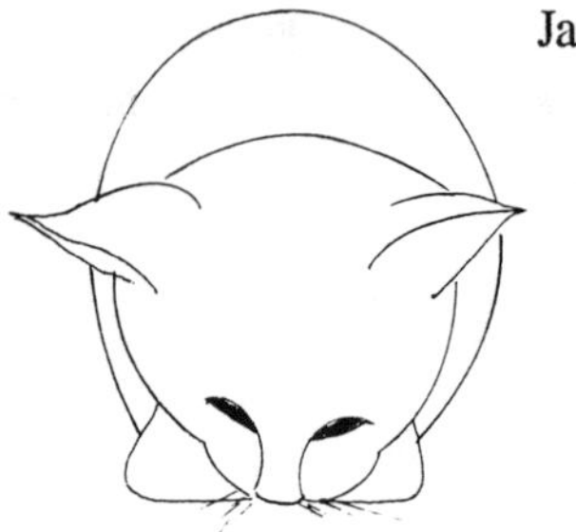

(x2)

THE OUTSIDER

Four cats we have of our very own who adopted us years ago,
But lurking in the underbrush is a fifth one that we know.
Though he's tried for months and months to join our happy troupe,
Our four will not permit another member in the group.

A lovely creature, but he's tough and really not refined,
So the limits our four set for him are strict and well defined.
The garden in the large back yard is clearly their preserve,
The gate from it out to the front the range he must observe.

Though the gate's a solid one, it has a cat-hole down below;
This is so our own four cats can freely come and go.
As long as Foxie—that's his name—remains outside the gate,
Our four, it seems, are quite content to let him sit and wait.

When Foxie crouches at his hole, waits anxiously for food,
He's found a strong defensive spot to keep at bay our brood.
Horatius Cocles at the Roman Bridge, and Foxie at his gate,
Both set fine examples we all appreciate.

Foxie knows his place quite well, he stays beyond the pale
As long as I alert remain and feed him without fail,
But if by chance I'm running late and don't appear on time,
Foxie ventures through the hole, a heinous feline crime!

As our four come down to sup, each one growls at him;
I quickly have to intervene, prevent a conflict grim.
A sign from me and Foxie turns and runs back through his hole,
While our own defensive four to the kitchen I now cajole.

When all of ours have gulped their meal, they run back whence they came,
Leaving Foxie beyond the pale, sitting there just the same.
As I approach with a dish of food, he emits some plaintive cries,
They are just faint croaking squeaks no matter how he tries.

His voice is almost non-existent, a mystery to us;
He simply lacks the vocal chords required to make a fuss.
I doubt that we shall ever learn what happened to his voice;
To find himself in such a state was surely not his choice.

Though Foxie still remains outside and waits there by his hole,
He's won a place quite near our heart, he's such a handsome soul.
We'd like to take him fully in and treat him like the rest,
But at least we try to feed him well, provide him with the best.

May 16, 1993

PERSUASION

A seething mass before the door,
A silent hungry mob.
You really couldn't ask for more
To get you on the job.

You know their need, their emptiness.
Though they were filled just hours before,
Their gnawing pangs to help suppress
Is now your major chore.

Just open a can from the stack on hand
And dish it out posthaste,
Your response to their demand.
Let's hope it suits their taste.

But if they sniff and walk away
To see to other affairs,
Their rejection spoils your day
But does not trouble theirs.

Soon back they come and truff right in,
More hungry than before.
Just open up another tin,
You know they'll want some more.

And that's the role you have to play:
You yield to ev'ry whim.
When cats come 'round and choose to stay,
You learn to humour them.

Jan. 8, 1993

RAIN

In they rush, it's time to eat;
My, what a nasty night!
Matted fur, ratty tails,
They really are a sight!

Dry 'em off and brush 'em down,
And let 'em sprawl about.
We'll feed 'em well and warm 'em up
Before they go back out.

Cats to the left, cats to the right,
Tails aloft with pride,
Swapping kisses, rubbing noses,
Ready to go outside—
To watch the rain.

Months and months of drought each year
Makes rain for them a treat;
When once they learn they've naught to fear,
They think it's kinda neat.

Each winter though, they learn anew
Just what that wondrous rain can do:
It wets their feet and cleans their claws,
But when it pours it gives them pause.

They love to sit in windows dry
And gaze out on the storm.
You can't believe how hard they try
To take this for the norm.

But sunny days soon come again;
For months and months they stay.
The cats adjust to lack of rain,
Content to sleep and play.

And when at last the rains return,
The glorious heaven-sent balm,
It gives again the chance to learn
The sheer delight of summer's calm.

So they sit inside and watch the rain
And meditate and muse,
The racing drops upon the pane
Their dreams will not confuse.

The winter rain, how well they know,
It teaches ev'ry one
How blessed is the chance to glow
Out in the summer sun.

Dec. 29, 1992

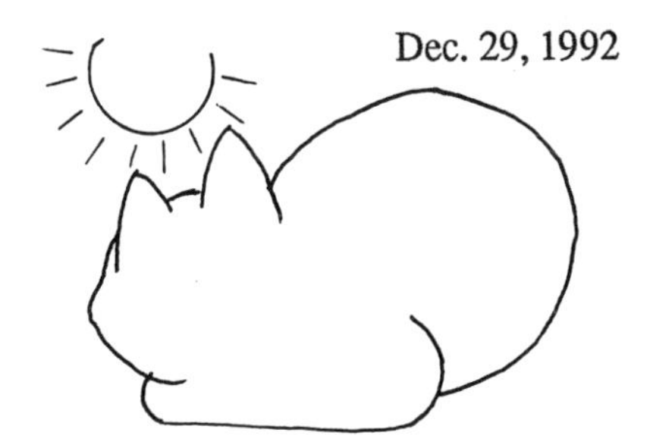

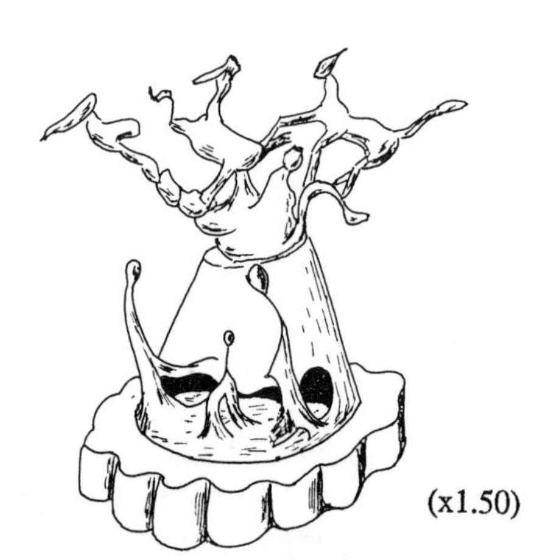

(x1.50)

SALLIES FROM THE ALLEY*

Oh, you can search along the beach at Bali Bali,
Or in continental gardens most sublime,
But the cats you'll likely find out in the alley
Are the ones with which I wish to spend my time.

No, they surely aren't too fancy or exotic,
Not descended from some really royal line,
But if you yourself are calm and unquixotic,
They'll settle in and fit your lifestyle fine.

We have four of them that came into our precints,
Three kittens that their Mum was pleased to share.
I suppose that she was guided by her instincts
To bring them in and have them settle there.

And though at first they seemed to be a nuisance
That cluttered up our lives, got in the way,
We soon began to find it gave a new chance
To change our pace, reorganize our day.

So now we've settled down, become a part of them;
They organize the way they'd have us go.
They've got us so we yield to ev'ry whim,
And make us feel we like to have it so.

These sallies from the alley bring us fresh delight:
They keep us on our toes throughout the day.
But, best of all, their antics in the night
Help us as we try to keep deep sleep away.

(Of course, I must correct a deadly misconception:
The males should not be labelled Sallies,
But, please, excuse this paronomasic deception,
Hoping the rest with sense and reason tallies.)

They like to sleep with us when'er the nights are cold:
That to you may sound a perfect scheme.
The truth, I fear, when all the facts are told,
Is that it's best to sleep alone and dream.

Perhaps the proper place for cats is alleys,
Perhaps they're best for all left in the wild,
But, I must confess that cats' domestic sallies
Have appealed to me since I was but a child.
And always will.

Jan. 5, 1993

*May be sung to the tune of *The Beach at Bali Bali*, which suggested the first line and the overall rhythmic pattern of the poem.

SISSY WAS A GENTLEMAN

When Mum her kittens three laid down upon our backdoor stoop,
Our task was first to find some names that suited all the troupe.
No matter at this early stage just how much time you take,
Both boys for girls and girls for boys it's easy to mistake.

The smallest of the three was surely not a male,
The gentlest of the three a lady without fail.
The third and last was big but just a mother's boy;
He stayed right close beside her and always acted coy.

The smallest was, indeed, a female that we'd got,
Although she grew to be the fiercest of the lot.
The gentlest of the three, at first we called her Sis,
Turned out to be a gentleman–in truth he was no miss!

The third, of course, was as we thought: a bouncing baby Tom,
Although he almost never left the shelter of his Mom.
Our batting, then, was not too bad; we'd got two out of three:
A little girl, so neat and prim, two boys for company.

The problem then was what to call the one that was misnamed,
An error in anatomy for which we now are blamed.
We'd change the name from Sis to Ses and hope he wouldn't mind.
(Ses is short for Cecil, but it seems to suit him fine.)

So Ses he was and Ses he'll be, he seems to like it well;
The change has done no harm to him, so far as we can tell.
He knows his name and seems quite proud to have it thus applied;
We found him one that met the need. How glad we are we tried!

Dec. 20, 1992

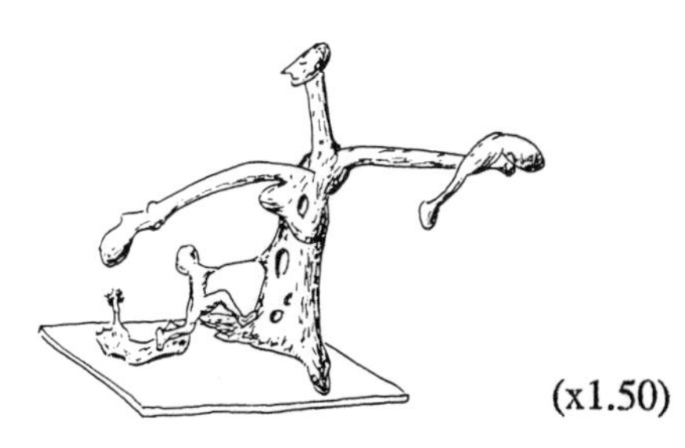

(x1.50)

THE SLINGS AND ARROWS OF OUTRAGEOUS FATE

My mealtime companion, the bride of my youth, has now been displaced by a cat.
Whenever it's raining or cold outside, he comes and lies down where she sat.
I find it great fun at mealtimes to watch the contest that often ensues
When Wedgie comes in and flops in her chair, our own meal plans to confuse.

He never considers her needs at all; as soon as his meal is done
He leaps to her chair for his post-prandial wash, and this is the start of the fun.
He's quite unconcerned over the trouble he's caused, his job now to clean himself well,
Then after that it's time for a nap, so he settles right down for a spell.

But what of my wife, my own poor spouse, and what of the meal she'd planned?
Why she sits on the stairs in the living room and holds her plate in her hand.
I sit there, too, just one step below, balancing my plate on my knee;
As we sit on the stairs enjoying our meal, it's a comical sight to see.

To suffer the arrows and slings that are cast in our lives by outrageous fate
Is an answer to the question that Shakespeare posed as we move with our meal and our plate:
Thought's pale cast has indeed sickled o'er the hue of our own resolution,
And we as cowards to conscience have bowed, yielding to weak constitution.

But I think you'd concur if you saw that cat, comfortably snoozing away,
That this, as we move through our twilight years, is a very small price to pay.
His peace is unmarred by the dread and fear of humans larger than he,
One of the smaller of nature's wee orbs, a contentment delightful to see.

April 17, 1993

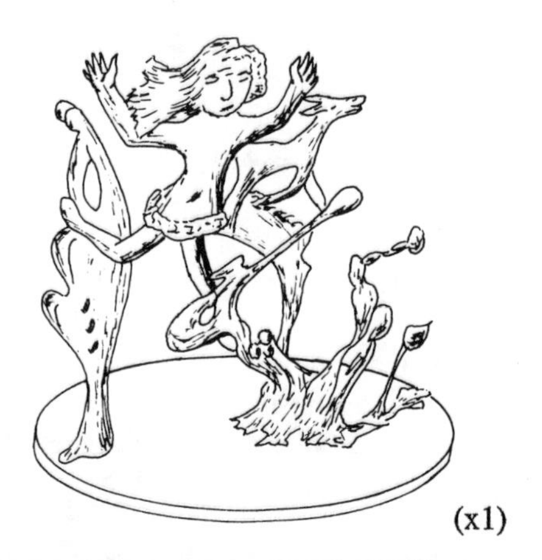

(x1)

SOMNIOCLASTIC AILUROPHILIA

Ailurophilic somnioclasy for some is quite a curse;
To sleep alone—no cat at all—for others is even worse.
Ailurophilous somnoclasy may make the ictus shift,
But even with this subtle change we still can catch the drift:

(It has to do with cats and sleep and how the two interact.)

What's to show for a night undisturbed, devoted to unbroken sleep?
Of course you feel rested and ready for work, thanks to your slumber so deep,
But what can you show for your time spent in bed if sleeping is all that you've done?
If you weren't kept awake by a cat wanting out, you just haven't had any fun.

You've written no poems, no music sublime, you've drawn not a picture at all;
No metrical verse, no new song to sing, nothing to hang on the wall.
By staying awake for an hour or two you might have produced an idea
That would create one of these, pleasant to see or delightful to hear.

Man's cultural treasure you'll surely enhance by investing some nocturnal hours.
To develope a skill, increase creativity, improve on some God-given powers,
Nature conspires with a cat and your age, insomnia's the happy result,
A chance to use time you'd have lost in sleep, just cause, indeed, to exult.

My fate was determined when long-haired Ces decided with me he would sleep.
He insists I retire as soon as he does, a rendezvous I must keep.
He's ready by seven to trot off to bed, but I'm expected to do the same;
I cover his head to keep out the light—it's all a part of the game.

The night starts well as I read or write with the slumbering cat at my side.
'Twould be hard to find a happier scene, no matter how you tried.
Then by ten I'm ready to sleep, three hours of slumber sublime,
For just after one old Ces wakes up, for him it's cleaning time.

He licks and he washes for a half hour or more—needless to say, I'm awake—
Now he's ready to go downstairs, partake of a wee-hour sup.
In somnambulant state I place him and his food outside the kitchen door
And hasten up to my nice warm bed, hoping to sleep now some more.

But, of course, by now I'm quite wide awake, Morpheus has taken flight;
The cat and his antics have intervened and shattered my plans for the night.
So I take out my papers and start in to write—a great time to work on my book!
A chance to retrieve the slumberless hours that feline companionship took.

Dec. 31,1992

THE USES OF FELINE ADVERSITY

The night is at peace, the house all asleep,
The cat is tucked in at your side.
What could be better than slumber so deep?
But that's for the cat to decide.

As you lie there in comfort next to each other
You can dream of the bliss of life's cup.
This is your plan, but the cat has another:
He thinks it is time to get up.

What do you do when your cat gets you up
At two in the morning with frost on the ground?
He decided he'd like warm milk and a sup,
Perhaps some nice fish could be found.

As he sits there at ease, at breakfast sublime,
Too early to heat up the house,
What can you do to best use the time?
It's surely no good to sit there and grouse.

Conditions are perfect to use, it would seem,
The time that you have on your exercise scheme,
And while you're immersed in your twistings and bends,
You're surely, indeed, making healthy amends.

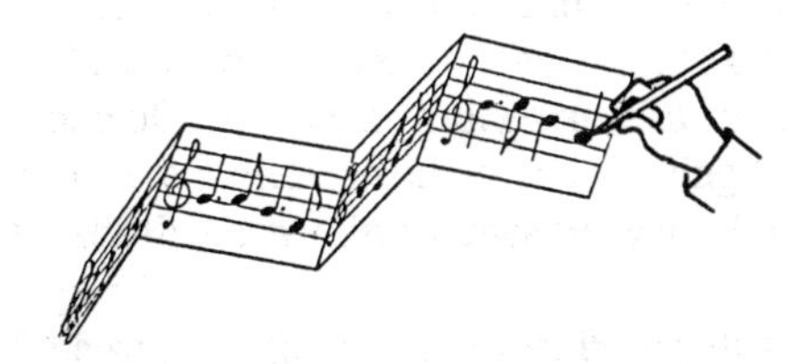

Now you're awake, the cat is replete
And ready his night to complete,
What do you do as he lies there and snores?
Any useful pursuits, any worthwhile chores?

The time is ideal some song to compose,
Some work 'til you're ready to doze,
Or, perhaps, you can sketch the slumbering cat,
So easy to do when he's still like that.

And then there are letters you've wanted to write:
Your brain will work well in the still of the night.
Oh, it's an excellent time to be used by a poet
Or someone so skilled who doesn't yet know it.

When plans go awry, just start out afresh,
And change your gears 'til they mesh.
Muster your own innate diversity,
But never given in to adversity.

Jan. 6, 1993

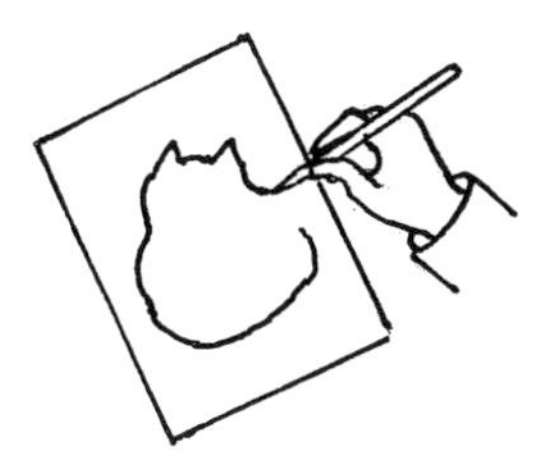

WHERE, OH, WHERE DOES CECIL GO?

Where all day does Cecil go?
To the neighbor's house where silkies grow.
He dashes home for ev'ry meal,
But after that we've no appeal.

Back he trots, across the street,
There to find his day complete.
What he does we still don't know,
We can but watch and see him go.

Perhaps he likes their flowing tresses,
Delights to watch such tiny messes.
He's twice the size of each of them,
His coat, though long, is far more trim.

Perhaps he finds companionship
Waits for him on ev'ry trip,
Though here at home we try to show
Him ev'ry kindness that we know.

He's still a creature proud and free,
Whose secret life we'll never see.
He takes from us just what he wants,
And then he's off to favored haunts.

But now we've reached a compromise:
For him, no change, for us, surmise.
And so he goes his merry way;
Perhaps quite soon he'll come to stay.

Dec. 21, 1992

Part TWO

THE ARMY

Do you object, as, I confess, I do,
To a page as blank as this *verso* ought to be?
To maculate the immaculate, unblank
The *verso* blank would seem a worthy task,
But one with danger fraught, for nought appalls
Much more than splotchy sublimation.

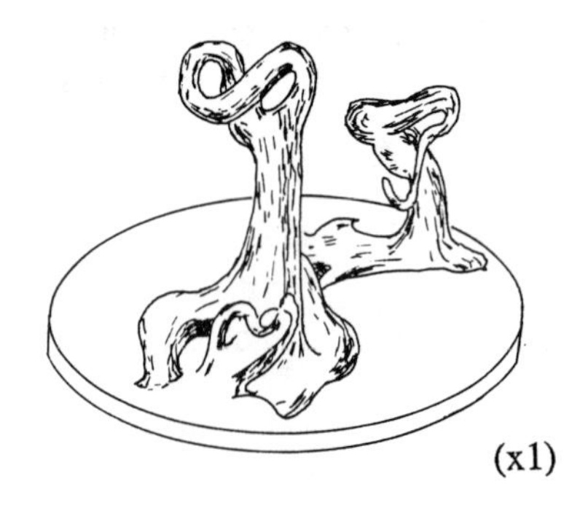

(x1)

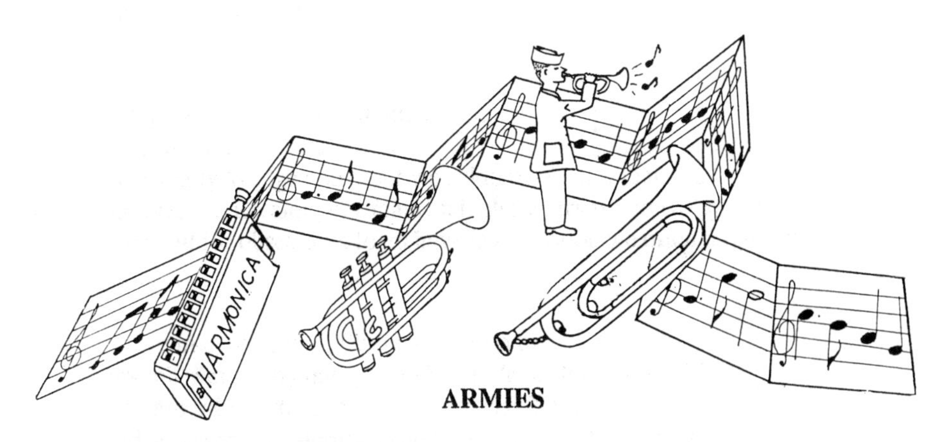

ARMIES

I've served in two armies at times in my life, each with its own attributes.
Let's think for a moment of the mission of each, of the foes that each one confutes.
The first one I joined as quite a young man, when the world in a war was embroiled;
The second I joined at 60 or so, and in it since then I have toiled.

The first was the army of the United States, the time was World War II.
I left my research and studies behind for a life somewhat different and new,
Though the training I'd had in old academe was ideal for my newfound career,
And my music, of course, could also fit in in ways abundantly clear.

The weapons I used were the same as at school: microscopes, stains, and pipettes.
To find myself busy with well-known tasks left me with no real regrets.
The army was using the skills that I had, and my pals were all college men,
So soon we began to feel quite at ease, like students in school once again.

I surely must mention the role music played in this, my new army life,
For it helped me evade some of the stress with which the army was rife.
Of course it was natural that I should become the bugler wherever I went,
This in return for the toil and sweat on my lovely cornet I had spent.

And then the piano paved the way, the chromatic harmonica, too,
To brighten the hours and lighten the load of jobs we had to do.
Music for me was a godsend, indeed; it cheered up many a day;
Oh, what a joy when the day's work was done to flee with my music and play.

But what of the second of those armies I served? Indeed, was it much like the first?
What was the type of desire that I had, what was the source of my thirst?
It all came about from a physical state that almost did me in,
But the miracle of modern medical science gave me my life back again.

Early retirement from teaching I took, with arteries hardened too soon,
But this I now know in retrospect was really a blessing, a boon.
I was forced to reduce the pace of my life, to develope in other ways,
To spend lots more time with the music I loved, a fine way to lengthen my days.

Music it was that helped me to join the second of the armies I've served:
The Salvation Army, that has as its goal the soul of men to preserve
From sin's degradation and all it entails, total destruction of life;
An army that's striving to strengthen the weak, save them from tension and strife.

They needed a pianist to play for their choir; I was happy to volunteer
To join an army with such noble ideals, with goals so radiantly clear.
As the years roll by and energies wane, I struggle to find proper ways
Of helping the army achieve its goal through my declining days.

With my computer I now can write books, hopefully peddle a few,
And give the returns to the Salvation Army to help with the work that they do.
This way I can use the time that is left to ends that I feel are worthwhile,
And when the time comes to say "Goodbye", I can do so with a smile.

April 26, 1993

(x1.50)

THE ARTFUL DODGERS

Pennsylvania snow was quite a shock for a lad from the southern sun;
The army's plan for its G.I.'s was to see such mixing done.
As we awaited a ship to take us abroad, the army was faced with a chore:
How to keep busy ten thousand men and next week ten thousand more?

The sergeants all tried to think up jobs to keep us occupied,
But to evade such tasks, avoid their work, ev'ry trick we G.I.'s tried.
Goldbricks were quite commonplace, many turned up sick;
False errands and excuses, too, the smart ones made them stick.

One gloomy morn as we lay abed, communing with the inner man,
An artist friend from New York land came up with a lovely plan:
The officer's mess was just the place to paint some pictures bright;
We'd sleep all day to regain our strength and then we'd paint all night.

Our sergeant thought the plan was sound and passed it on up high,
Where paints and brushes soon appeared, so we could have a try.
That night at ten, when all the other troops had gone to bed,
The three of us began to paint, just as we had said.

Only one of us was trained in art, the other two were not;
Our leader, though, knew how to use the modest skills we'd got:
A drafting course I once had had, so a straight line I could make;
The third man once in grammar school a class in crafts did take.

The scheme we used was simple and neat, the pace we set was good:
Insignia of ev'ry unit we found and painted all we could.
The artist pencilled out each one, with numbers for the colors:
Red and blue and green and yellow, there really were no others–
But black and white, of course.

Night after night the three men worked, they brightened up the place;
The officers all seemed pleased indeed at the vigour of their pace.
To cap it off the kitchen crew, that cooked and baked all night,
Would let the three eat heartily of ev'rything in sight.

So, by the time the ship arrived to take them overseas,
The three were fat, the hall was bright, the project seemed to please.
The story goes to show, I think, that artful dodgers, too,
At times of gloom, in peace or war, do have a job to do.

Feb. 8, 1993

THE ART OF WAR

Reams have been written on the art of war, but, please, let me add by bit,
For it shows a much happier side of it all and the tricks in the soldier's kit.
The scene was laid far overseas, where warriors convalescent
Could heal their wounds, regain their strength, and then go back to their regiment.

Dozens and dozens of Nissen huts were scattered about the camp,
Each with a stove and its own pile of coke to keep out the cold and damp.
Many were bleak and dingy and dark, the windows were small and shut,
But one stood out from all the rest, we called it The Artist's Hut.

The men who ran it could draw and paint, their colors made it bright:
With pretty pictures on the walls, it was a lovely sight.
They did their best to make the camp a cheery place to be,
With lots of signs and posters bright for one and all to see.

After hours, when work was done, the hut was a busy place;
For chaps who liked to sketch and draw, 'twas a welcome change of pace.
What a happy scene it was, remote from guns and strife,
Though splints and casts galore there were, and crippled limbs were rife.

From ev'ry part of the USA they came and gathered there;
Some to paint, some to draw, some to just sit and stare.
Some were content to work alone, creating their own piece of art,
But others tried to teach a pal to acquire the skill to start.

A little sculptor from the Bronx, modelling a horse in clay,
While a Spanish galleon, its sails unfurled, prepared to sail away.
A taxidermist, with special skills he'd learned as a youth out west,
Was helping two young southern lads make a squirrel look its best.

Paints and brushes, pencils and pads, clay and wax, and gesso too:
An excellent way to forget one's wounds, raise one's spirits anew.
The hut was truly a haven for them, a place where their thoughts could roam
As they worked on a masterpiece and dreamt a bit of home.

Here at least for a little while the men were able to dream,
Free to develope a creative idea, however wild it might seem.
Here they could express an inner urge to make a thing of beauty,
Free from the rigours of army life, free from the call of duty. (April 8, 1993)

THE BUGLE TRILOGY

I

THE BUGLE AT DAWN

Long years ago of an English morn
The air was rent by a G.I.'s horn
In a word at war the day began
With a sprightly tune from the music man.

The soldiers bold were loath to rise
And start the day 'neath pre-dawn skies.
But rise they must to the trumpet's blast
To do their job and do it fast.

The slumb'ring village round about
Had the grace and charm to pretend
That such a racket that brought them out
Could only be made by a friend.

So they'd cover their heads and seek release
By dreaming once more of post-war peace,
For it still was true that the horn of the Yanks
Was better by far than Hitler's tanks.

Dec. 24, 1992

II

THE BUGLE CALL

Young lungs that swelled and blew a horn
To wake the troops on an English morn,
Now old and frail, have lost their zest,
A whistled call is now their best.

In days gone by, when they were strong
To sound a summons loud and long,
The task they did was really needed,
The calls they blew were always heeded.

At dawn they'd cause the men to rise
And start to work 'neath still-dark skies.
All day they'd chase 'em round and about,
Replacing many a sergeant's shout.

And then at last, when day was done,
The call would sound for ev'ry one
To heed again the last refrain
And settle back to bed again.

But now the call is a whistled call
Sounding forth for cats—that's all.
But still it's done with joy and pride
In answer to an urge inside.

The whistled call is loud and clear,
It summons cats from far and near,
Not only ours, their yard to defend,
But all the neighbors', foe and friend.

So on it goes 'til lungs collapse;
It's hard to stop these noisy chaps.
Old bugler's never die, they say,
They just dry up and blow away.

And blow, and blow, and blow....

Dec. 25, 1992

(x2)

III

THE BUGLER'S ORDEAL

In a world at war in forty-three, some bright spots yet appeared;
England to a lots of Yanks became a land endeared:
The hills, the fields, the people too—I married one of them.
This tale I tell of a bugler there and what became of him.

Each day at dawn, rain or shine, he had to rise and blow his horn;
No band there was, so he alone would brighten up the morn
With bugle calls and lots of songs the G.I.'s all would know;
It helped to start the day off well to hear the fellow blow.

One ominous day, the sergeant came, portentous news he brought:
The bugling was of some concern, by the captain the bugler was sought.
To this officer stern, report he did and was told he must now go
To see a spavined general about the morning's blow.

He was ushered in to the general's room, the old man lay abed,
Stern and fierce, indeed, he looked, the youngster almost fled.
With shaky knees he stood erect, saluted as was right,
Waited, braced, for the awful storm of all the general's might.

As he stood all tense, through his head there raced all sorts of nameless fears:
Would he lose his stripe, his music, too; how could he face his peers?
The general, too, was tense indeed, not once did he relax
As he prepared the bugler there with his morning deeds to tax.

The strain was strong, the tension fierce, the young man near collapse;
No way he knew to make his escape or evade the general's traps.
But just as he neared the breaking point, he saw on the general's face
A smile appear, his eyes light up, a hand extend with grace.

The old man reached across the bed and said "Shake hands, young man;
The bugler's role is a happy one, I like the army plan!
I myself, when I started out, bugled the lads from their sleep;
I, for one, am quite convinced that buglers we should keep.

I hate a post where bugle calls are blared out taped or canned;
Give me a camp where I see the horn and see it really manned."
The two of them, bugler's both, an old one and a new,
Chatted there for quite a while about things buglers do.

A bright spot in the day, indeed, and music made it so;
From this delightful confrontation they both would happier go.
The joy the general gave that day to the young man at his side
Has lasted now for fifty years, a constant source of pride.

Jan. 31, 1993

AN ENGLISH CHRISTMAS

I well remember forty-three, a rainy Christmas Day;
The cook gave me a box of lunch and sent me on my way.
A fossil site some distance off was where I'd hoped to go:
What types of fossils there I'd find, I really didn't know.

A stood out on the roadside dark—the day was still pitch black—
When all at once a car drove past but turned and then came back.
The driver kindly picked me up and asked me home with him;
An air-raid warden, he'd spent his night on rooftops wet and grim.

I met his wife and children too, we talked of many things;
I saw that day true family love, the happiness it brings.
They made me promise when I left that I'd return and share
Their Christmas meal without fail, they'd all be waiting there.

So out into the rain I went to find the fossil bed;
I filled a bag with fossil shells, and on the army lunch I fed.
But soon 'twas time to turn away and go back to that home
With four good English friends I'd made this day I chose to roam.

They welcomed me with open arms, and dinner soon appeared;
The children then a gesture made that them to me endeared:
It seems that they had spent their day making gifts for me;
I'm sure that they could never know how deeply touched I'd be.

That Christmas Day of all I've known, stands out above the rest,
Because to me it seems to show true Christian love the best:
A total stranger there I was, but the love that poured from them
Brings Christ the Saviour to my mind and the love we have from him.

Feb. 13, 1993

THE GENERAL'S PINKS

My lot in the army was quite a lucky one;
I had a lot of challenges, and lots of them were fun.
My Irish luck I guess it was, I really cannot say,
But something always did turn up in time to save the day.

Several times events transpired I couldn't understand;
Things worked out quite differently from anything I'd planned.
To win the war I went abroad to help support the side;
While others won the war, I won an English bride.

Looking through a microscope was how I fought the war,
Though it's really not the sort of work they gave you medals for.
I got a commendation that I surely had not earned,
For at two o'clock one morning, the general's pinks I'd burned.

The story is a simple one of gross incompetence.
The general came in late that night, the fog outside was dense,
My captain from the lab me pulled to act as orderly,
My task to keep the general neat and looking soldierly.

When I tucked him into bed, I now could have a chance
To dash back to the lab and press his wrinkled pants.
An iron I borrowed from a nurse and took the task in hand,
But after that, disaster struck: it wasn't what I'd planned.

I must have got the iron too hot or let it rest too long,
For suddenly a stench arose that seemed to me quite wrong.
A horrible streak of dark brown cloth lay there before my eyes;
At two A.M. it was, I fear, a terrible surprise.

I did my best to get it out with ev'ry trick I knew,
But soon the truth became quite clear: 'twas more than I could do.
I went to sleep and nightmares had of years in army clinks
Just because I was inept and burned the general's pinks.

At eight A.M. I woke him up and helped him to get dressed;
His paunch concealed the inseam scorch on the trousers I had pressed.
I sent him off and held my breath to see what he would do
When once he found the mess I'd made of his lovely pinks so new.

The days went by and I returned to lab and microscope;
My sergeant thought my doom was sealed, I really had no hope,
But then that commendation came for service that I'd done:
Indeed, again, my army lot had been a happy one!

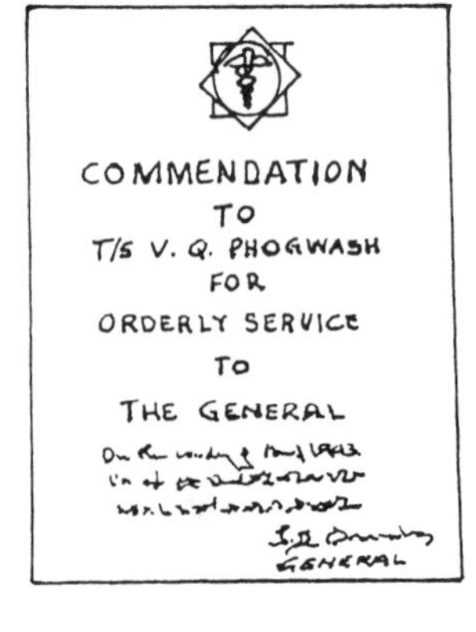

Feb. 17, 1993

G.I.'S AND THEIR BICYCLES

Site a large camp six miles away from the nearest English town;
There try to get eight hundred Yanks to quietly settle down.
No gas, no cars, no motored wheels at all; oh, tell me what the lonely guys could do?
They bought up all the bikes they could, though few of them were new.

Two pedals, two wheels, and an old rusty frame for some was all the bike was,
But to others who cared it gave them the chance to rig 'em out fancy like cars.
Lights front and back, reflectors galore, and even a racoon tail,
A horn and a bell, a sheepskin seat: your own you could tell without fail.

Alas and alack! They couldn't get paint in a land by war made austere,
So what money they had for painting their bikes they spent instead on beer.
A beery Yank on an English bike was a sight quite fine to see,
As he pedalled about through the countryside as happy as could be.

A favorite trick of many a Yank was riding without a light,
A very dangerous thing, of course, on a blacked out English night.
Perhaps he felt a broken leg or even an arm or two
Was mild, indeed, when one compared what Hitler's tanks could do.

When an English Bobby lifts his hand and softly calls out "stop!",
A proper English citizen quite fast obeys the cop,
But when the Bobby tries the same on a Yank who has no light,
He often finds the cussed Yank at once resorts to flight.

Of course it's hard to follow him: on foot he has no chance
To do much more than cast at him a hasty fleeting glance.
The odds are stacked against the law, no motorcycle cops were there.
The sort of trick theYank had pulled no Englishman would dare.

Next day to our camp, of course, the Bobby came around
To see if in our horde the felon could be found.
With hundreds of G.I.'s lined up, alike in their fatigues,
The Bobby had to give it up and so did his colleagues.

Stealing bikes was all the rage, there were so few for sale;
If ever you got caught, of course, you'd surely go to jail.
Some of the Yanks preferred that fate to tackling Hitler's tanks,
But for the trouble they caused us all, from us they got no thanks.

More than once we all were lined up as an Englishman slowly walked by
To see if in that motley lot a culprit he could spy.
I don't recall they found a one, or that the bike reappeared,
But by the lineup we at least from any crime were cleared.

In the communal life of an army camp, the life of a private wasn't private at all;
His bike alone was the only thing that the lad his own he could call.
He showered on it the love and the care that at home he had given his car,
For freedom it gave to his roaming soul to escape and go wandering far.

For an hour or two, perhaps even more, he could dream the world was at peace;
He could put out of mind the horrors ahead or from those he had seen get release.
The bike was his chance to be free for a while, to be just himself once again,
To forget about killing and the arts of war and think about things more humane.

So here's to the bike and here's to the men to whom they meant so much!
They helped them forget their role in the war, rekindle their human touch.
A statue I'd like to see them erect of a G.I. and his bike;
I think that would be more pleasing to see than one of Churchill or Ike.

Feb. 26, 1993

THE G.I.'S AND THE SWAN

The days were long in our hospital camp for soldiers convalescent;
Leaves were short or not at all, and joys were evanescent.
The camp was far from any town, amusements then were rare,
But a river small flowed by the camp, and lovely swans swam there.

One day into our lab there came a group of soldiers three:
A rope one had, a bag another, the third came up to me
And asked the loan of a new fire axe to help them kill a bird.
I thought it all a monstrous joke, the story quite absurd.

The axe they took, the rope, the bag, and off they disappeared;
The mission planned soon proved to be far worse than we had feared.
A fourth appeared, disclosed the plan: their quarry was a swan!
That swans were sacred to the king had caused them no alarm.

They'd lasso one and reel him in and dump him in the bag;
Once they got him back to camp, the axe would kill their swag,
And then they'd get the cook for them a lovely meal to make
With swan and beer and powdered eggs, and then, at last, some cake.

The spokesman for the three confessed that though they'd caught the beast,
His grace and beauty charmed them all, on him they'd never feast.
They turned him loose and watched their swan, rejoicing to be free;
Now ev'ry day those four G.I.'s feeding swans you see.

Jan. 31, 1993

(x1)

GREAT MILITARY CRISES I SURVIVED
A BELLICOSE TRILOGY

I

THE G.I. MALAISE

The pharmacy sergeant was out on a pass, and I was left in charge;
His usual task on a normal night was seldom very large.
One room was all the pharmacy had, the others all were the lab's;
They left me quite alone that night, my task on it all to keep tabs.

I wasn't trained as a pharmacist, though sometimes I studied their book;
That's why the sergeant left me in charge: he thought I could do what it took
For and hour or two—three at the most—while he popped out for a beer.
How could he have known at all that a terrible disaster was near?

As I sat all alone in the lab that night, happy at the big microscope,
In camp a crisis was developing fast with which I would soon have to cope.
A meal was served, the troops were fed, and ev'rything seemed just great,
But misery profound was soon to appear from something not right that they ate.

It all started out when up to the lab one soldier, the first to appear,
Came to the pharmacy seeking relief 'cause he said that he had diarrhoea.
By chance I knew well what to give the poor guy (the pharmacist had told me before),
But ere I was done with helping this one, six more appeared at the door.

I dealt with the six as fast as I could and rushed for the telephone
To call for the sergeant to come back at once, I just couldn't cope all alone.
He abandoned his beer, hopped on his bike, and pedalled for all he was worth,
And all encountered as he tore through the night gave him a truly wide berth.

By the time he got back, the scene he beheld was really quite ghastly, indeed:
The medicine we had was dwindling fast, and soon a lot more we would need.
The floor of the lab was a seething mass of soldiers wracked by pain;
Many of them feared that this was the end, they'd never see daylight again.

The sergeant was calm, knew just what to do: he mixed up gallons of stuff;
We passed it around to each one there and ev'ryone soon had enough
To settle their tums and realize they'd live, it wasn't their last night on earth.
How wondrous to see those G.I.'s exchange their gloom for a vestige of mirth!

Mar. 3, 1993

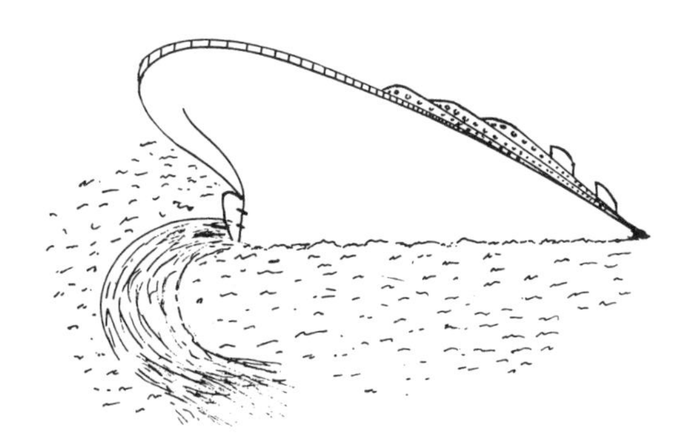

THE NIGHT THE QUEEN TURNED HER RIGHT ANGLE

From ev'rywhere west of the eastcoast ports the troop trains were rolling along:
Some of the guys were filled with remorse, others with laughter and song;
Most were too tired from the long trip they'd made to think of adventures ahead,
Though most of them knew that before 'ere long many would surely be dead.

As they sped through the night on the blacked-out train, they didn't know where they were,
But that a long sea voyage had been arranged for each, on that they all could concur.
Uncle Sam had equipped them all well, the trains were packed to the brim
With soldiers, their packs, gas masks, and all the weapons of war so grim.

And then at last, after days on the train, this phase of their journey was done.
They next had to wait 'til their troopship arrived, their adventures had hardly begun!
Their wait wasn't long—a few days or so—when again, in the still of the night,
They were herded aboard another full train whose movements were kept out of sight.

They sped through the night for an hour or two and stopped in what seemed a great hall,
But when they descended and looked through the gloom, they saw that a ship was one wall.
And, oh, what a vessel that great ship was, the largest that sailed on the seas;
They'd planned her space well and used ev'ry inch: she could take a division with ease.

We marched to the ship and climbed up and up 'til topsides we finally reached
And settled right down with nothing to see: not a light the blackout breached.
We could but feel our way around, crawling about in the dark
To find a space for settling down and ourselves and our gear to park.

We tried to sleep as well as we could in a blanket and all of our clothes;
Most of the guys soon drifted away, a few of them muttering oaths.
In spite of it all the night soon passed, by morning we were well out to sea;
My only desire was to lie there and sleep; oh, I was as sick as I could be!

The plan was to sleep one night on deck, the next in a bunk down below.
How I got down to that bunk in the hold, never, I fear, will I know,
But once I lay down I made up my mind the deck no more would I see:
One night abunk, the next on the floor was just what was right for me.

The third night out was a mem'rable one, for the Queen made a right-angle turn
Which threw us all from our bunks to the floor for a reason we could not discern.
All through the trip, to outwit the subs, often her course she had changed,
But this one that night was so very abrupt we all thought she was deranged.

The crisis soon passed and didn't recur, we all survived it quite well,
But the story that night of the right-angle turn remains exciting to tell.
For some of us—the real lucky ones—who had no adventures at all,
It's the only tall tale we are able to tell of the horrible world-wide brawl.

Mar. 6, 1993

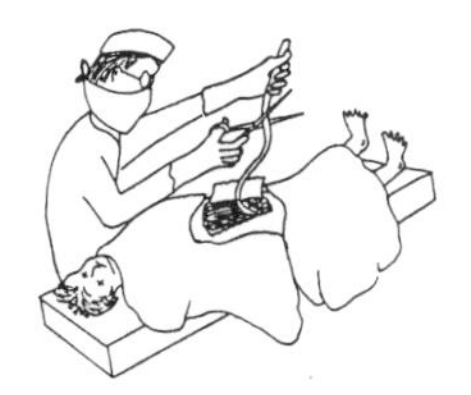

III

GUTS IN EXCESS

Gangrene, the scourge of World War One, caused far less trouble in World War Two.
The doctors' technique had improved quite a bit, far better they knew what to do.
The threat was still there, ready to pounce, waiting 'til conditions were right,
But when wounds were involved, the medics applied diligence day and night.

But sometimes the threat was not recognized, the symptoms weren't easy to spot:
No wounds were involved, the patient looked fine, although he did suffer a lot.
The only complaint the fellow could lodge were terrible stomach cramps;
He simply assumed he couldn't digest the food they served in the camps.

Many a night in the English hut that served as the soldier's latrine
He writhed on the floor—concrete and cold— with cramps that were terribly mean.
He didn't complain to the doctors he knew, he thought he had complained quite enough
With the headaches severe that caused such distress and proved quite often so tough.

After the war, the army disbanded, a family and profession ensued,
But the cramps in the stomach still his life with misery often imbued.
Many were the tests, many the exams, but still frequent the writhing pain:
As the years rolled by he simply despaired of ever being normal again.

But then one night the pain was so strong an ambulance took him away,
And a clever internist with a timely X-ray caught a bum colon at play.
With a colon too long, it got twisted up, and that is what caused all the pain;
If it ever stayed twisted and couldn't be released, the threat of gangrene was plain.

The need for surgery was immediate, indeed; they opened him up and removed
A foot and a half of intestinal tube, which left the chap greatly improved.
The threat of gangrene from wartime to peace was there all the time—but just latent—
Until a young doctor with X-rays he took made the threat to a life quite patent.

The chap in this story was I, I'm afraid, and the crisis was fifty years long,
So the purist might raise an objection and say for this case the word "crisis" is wrong,
But whatever the term one decides to use, I feel I was lucky indeed
To have survived all those years with an allotment of guts that exceeded my comfortable need.

Mar. 21, 1993

THE MISCREANTS

The Army had its rules, of course, supposed to be obeyed,
But G.I.'s, just to flaunt those rules, courage, skill, and wit displayed.
The officers were expected to apply the rules, but they usually knew their men:
They knew just when to give free reins or when to pull them in.

The sergeants, too, knew what was what, most secrets they did share,
And, through their innate guile and wit, the justice they upheld was fair.
They often looked the other way when the spirit of the law
Seemed to indicate to them the letter had a flaw.

And so it was that in the lab we often used xylene
To start a fire with English coke, a method fast and clean,
But one, no doubt, that broke a rule, or even two or three,
Though, fortunately for us, no officers came 'round to see.

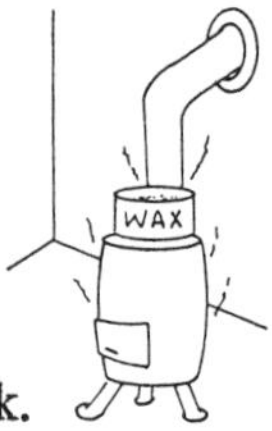

Another time our lawlessness caused lots of extra work.
This time the labor that ensued was such that none could shirk.
Gather 'round and listen well, but do not pass it on,
And I shall tell how disaster fell on a cold, bleak English morn.

A big inspection was due next day, with generals galore,
The sort of thing that most G.I.'s learned early to abhore.
We'd placed a can of cold floor wax upon the stove to melt,
When all at once impending doom with sickening clarity was smelt.

The can went up in flame and smoke— five gallons of burning wax!
To quench the flames and save the lab all our skill did tax,
But when at last the fire was out and the lab was cleared of smoke,
The results we saw and what they meant were clearly not a joke.

It meant we had to scrub all day and paint throughout the night,
To get the scum from off the walls and make them nice and bright.
But scrub we did and awake we stayed, we finished just at dawn,
And the only sign of the night's ordeal was an occasional stifled yawn.

The inspecting officers were pleased, indeed; they thought the lab looked fine.
They thought that to make it sparkle so was part of our grand design
To raise our standards, excell, and please beyond the letter of the law.
It's just as well our earlier frenzy was something they never saw.

April 2, 1993

THE MUSIC LOVERS

Oh, what respect the army had for culture of all sorts!
I'll never forget some sergeants we had and some of their cultural retorts!
Early one learned not to mention at all the subjects to one's heart most dear:
They'd only evoke relentless scorn or at least a heartfelt sneer.

Brahms and Bach were beyond the pale, for most they were simply unknown;
One's love for classical music, you see, was something they'd just not condone.
If you happened to like Ravel or Chopin, you had to subdue your desire
To play or to hear the music they wrote that kindled in you such a fire.

So it isn't surprising to hear a tale of a musical adventure I had
In the first few weeks of my army career, while I still was a fresh college lad.
I was so green I had not yet learned one rule to the G.I. most dear:
Wherever you go, whatever you do, remember, just don't volunteer.

The sergeant had called us out one day and lined us up in neat rows;
He had a campaign all mapped out, a secret he wouldn't disclose.
He simply requested the pianists among us to raise our hands and step out,
Which I did with alacrity along with some others, not knowing what it was about.

I could foresee some glorious event, a concert of noble mien,
Where we would all play the music we loved for an audience of listeners keen.
The army, indeed, was shaping up well, our future looked ever so bright
As we and the sergeant boarded a truck and swiftly rode off out of sight.

We came to a hall in the neighboring town and all eight of us went inside,
Where we saw a nice piano that each of us knew we'd be happy to play with pride.
As we stood and admired it, our fingers atwitch, we each wondered just what to play
At the concert they'd planned with us as the guests, pianists again for a day!

But then all at once our dreams were destroyed, as the sergeant stood there and roared:
"O.K., you guys, let's move that piano", shattering illusions that soared.
We heaved and we puffed and managed at last to get it aboard the truck,
Though getting it out when we got back to camp demanded considerable pluck.

But then at last, when we got it set up in the day room where all the guys came,
We each had a chance, though fleeting it was, to render some song that they'd name.
Not Bach or Chopin, but popular songs is all that they wanted to hear;
Something quite snappy to liven things up as they all sat around with their beer.

And that, I confess, is the fate that we faced as we entered our army career,
For popular songs in a light-hearted vein were things to the G.I. most dear.
This craving of theirs for songs that they knew inspired me to work on the style
And develop a skill to meet their needs and see it was really worth while.

I'd broken a rule, a basic one, too, that day when I volunteered
But it opened some doors in the army for me, and the way for real progress it cleared.
I soon was able my music to use by bugling, and then in a band
My cornet and piano provided a chance with music to take up my stand.

Whenever a chance to make music arose I offered to do so with glee.
The old army rule I broke many times, but I found it quite easy to see
That a volunteer's lot is a delightful one, if you know just what you're about.
That the army has room for culture of sorts I now know beyond any doubt.

April 24, 1993

MY MIDNIGHT PROWL AND THE CARDINAL RULE

I still remember my army days, though, yes, 'twas long ago;
Some things that come back to mind still today are fun to know.
My G.I. lot was a happy one, my mem'ries are mostly fond;
I even got an English bride across the Atlantic pond.

I never saw a battle field, I never fired a shot,
A microscope in England was the closest I ever got.
One of the lucky ones, indeed—there were lots of us—
We simply tried to do our job without a lot of fuss.

My first night in the service, though, I never shall forget:
Atlanta in December, 'twas cold and dark and wet.
Our barracks, too, were very large: a hundred men or more;
You'd not believe the stench of feet nor the volume of the snore.

Late that night, when the lights were out, I had an urge most keen
To tumble out, run through the dark to find a close latrine.
To find it was the easy part, to get back into bed was not;
A horrible task in the pitch-black dark to find my empty cot.

I had to crawl from bed to bed to try to find my own;
I little knew when I'd left that bed what seeds of toil I'd sown.
I stumbled over boots and shoes and clothes left on the floor,
Counting beds both left and right, mine wasn't near the door!

I must have crawled for half an hour before at last I found
My empty cot and got back in to resume my sleep so sound.
I learned a cardinal rule that night: it's wise to plan ahead
And always know exactly how to get back to your bed.

April 2, 1992

OUR MASCOT

The bright spot in war for many a G.I. was the music he was able to make;
Of the joy he spread his fellow G.I.'s were also able to partake.
At one camp in England before the invasion of Fortress Europa began,
A band from the camp played dances and such with a well-organized plan.

The band was assembled with all of its gear, a truck for them, too, commandeered.
They were eager to go, anxious to play, what was delaying the troupe?
Then out of the night—it was blackout, of course—a bark, a yip, and a small dog appeared;
The truck couldn't roll 'til the dog was aboard, an essential part of the group.

The driver jumped down and picked up the dog and lifted him in to the men;
Off the truck roared to the dance with them all: the band and its canine mascot.
To the dance hall they went, and the music could start as soon as the dog went in;
The audience well knew the pride of the band was that nondescript pooch they had got.

The English were jolly and so was the band, the music was brightened with beer;
As the evening wore on it was clear that the dance was enjoyed by everyone there,
But all would agree that the happiest of all in this crowd of joy and good cheer
Was the dog seated there with a saucer of beer, lapping it up on a chair.

After the dance, the bandsmen were tired, the truck had a slumbering load;
Snuggled among them, all cosy and warm, of course, was their canine pet.
The journey home was slow, indeed, through the fog on the blacked-out road,
But the load at the back was about as content as G.I.'s and a dog could get.

Feb. 3, 1993

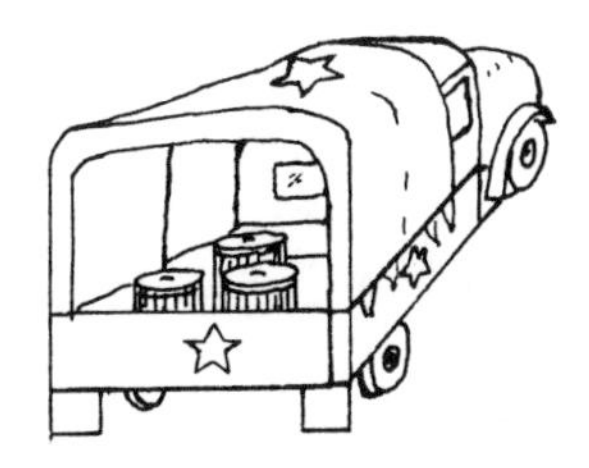

THE PECKING ORDER FOR YANKEE GARBAGE

Three thousand Yanks ate lots of food, but there also was lots of waste;
They had to eat whatever they took, no matter what its taste.
They weren't permitted to throw food away, they had to eat it all;
They had to devour each morsel of food before they left the hall.

The waste arose in the kitchen itself, mostly just food that was spoiled:
A crate of oranges with mold on a few, a few loaves of bread that were soiled.
The mess sergeants all had a morbid fear of the havoc bad food could wreak:
Mass diarrhoea could floor the camp, leave it all wan for a week.

The rule in the kitchen was to throw food away if its condition was in any doubt,
For upset tums and the problems they caused they best would all be without.
The kitchen crews were a compassionate bunch, they knew that life was tough,
That food in England was hard to get; there simply wasn't enough.

The camp had arranged with a farm nearby to send all its waste to the swine;
For the Yanks it was easy, the pigs were quite pleased, and the English thought it was fine.
Whenever a truck appeared from the camp excitement reigned at the farm,
And a message was sent to the village nearby to raise the joyous alarm.

For the cooks here saw an excellent chance to help their hungry allies;
It seemed such a pity to leave lots of food just sitting around for the flies.
So they'd add to the truck some food that was good under what seemed to be bad:
Oranges, apples, potatoes and eggs, whatever it was that they had.

The farm folk soon learned that all they must do was unload the stuff with great care,
Then dig down below the bad bits on top to find the good stuff that was there.
And what a great treat were these gifts from the Yanks, officially meant for the pigs:
Grapefruit and lemons, rolls and bread, bananas, tomatoes, and figs.

All sorts of things that in England were rare, made so by the old German sub,
Now appeared right out of the blue, discards from the great Yankee grub.
The farm folk went through it, took what they wanted, and summoned the village nearby,
Who came and pitched in to share the delights from the trucks of their Yankee ally.

P.O.W.'s were the next group to come: Germans at work on the land.
They joined in the fun with banter and smiles, they thought it all was quite grand.
When all the groups of humans were done, when they'd finished their various digs,
The stuff that was left—not very much—was then given out to the pigs.

An American Kaiser, Henry by name, with his shipyards so massive out west,
From the Kaiser's successor (Hitler abroad) was able to win the contest:
He was able to build ships faster, indeed, than Hitler could sink them at sea,
And that helps account for the story above, that's how it all came to be.

Mar. 30, 1993

THE PRIVATE'S RAT TERRIER AND
THE COLONEL'S GREAT DANE

Rank has its privileges, as all G.I.'s know; the private, of course, has few,
But let me tell you of a case, about a private I knew:
The scene is laid in an army camp in England in forty-four
Where injured soldiers were regaining their strength to go and fight some more.

Our colonel had a monstrous dog, and this was no surprise.
But then one day a miracle occurred, we could hardly believe our eyes!
Into the camp a truck appeared with a load of injured men:
They all would soon be well again, but no one knew just when.

Among the mass of crippled men who tumbled from the truck
Was a wee little dog—black and white—small but full of pluck.
Most of the soldiers were big and tall, but one was small and thin.
The little dog belonged to him, the smallest of the men.

We soon found out that the private with the dog was a master of piano and horn.
As soon as he played at rehearsal with us, it was obvious to music he was born.
So we made him a part of our small dance band— he did the work of two—
And all of the music we regularly played we found he already knew.

Delightfully, too, his dog came along and became a part of our crew,
And while we were playing for dances and such, just guess what the terrier would do:
He'd sit in a chair with a saucer of beer and have a fine time on his own;
No matter how long we stayed on the job, from him there was never a moan.

The Colonel's Great Dane led the life of a prince, a royal existence indeed!
His ev'ry desire was catered for, someone to meet ev'ry need,
But I suspect that the terrier that went with the band was the happier dog by far,
Without the constraints of officership his daily existence to mar.

He could roam through the camp with three thousand men, each his own special friend,
And then at a dance he knew he could drink: beer and more beer without end!
But the Colonel's Great Dane had to sit all day in an office so stuffy and smug,
And then at night stay in his kennel, stretched out asleep on his rug.

A little dog's life in a great camp like that was full of adventure and fun:
He could go to the river and bark at the swans or stay with the soldiers and run,
But the poor Great Dane must have found life dull, ev'rything all spick and span;
His daily routine must have been much the same since his career in the army began.

The little rat terrier had all the rats in the camp to chase when he pleased
And scores of technicians to watch over him, solicitous whenever he sneezed.
If I were a dog and then forced to choose between the lives of these two,
I'd prefer the rat terrier's to the monstrous Great Dane's, I'm sure 'tis the right thing to do.

Mar. 28, 1992

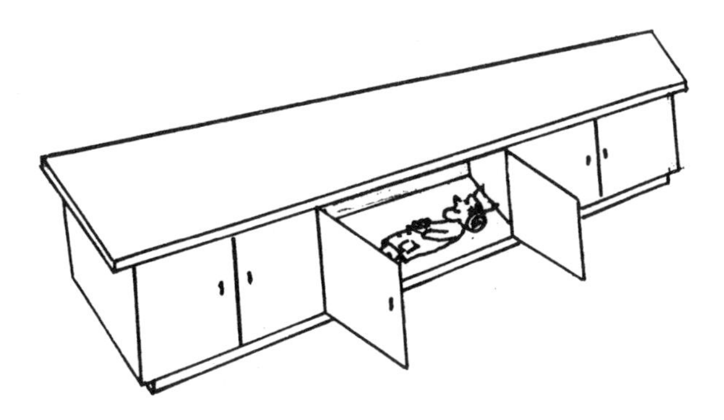

SLEEPING THROUGH INSPECTION

Inspections to the army always seemed to be the bread of life,
But for the lowly G.I. Joe they merely caused more strife.
Of all the inspections we hated most were those that weren't announced,
When on an error we had made some officer had pounced.

To find a way of avoiding such trials was a lively challenge for all;
It often made us concoct excuses and tell some tales quite tall.
A favorite trick for us in the lab was inspired by some cupboards we had:
They ran full length below the main desk—a great place for hiding a lad!

The lab never closed, it ran day and night, someone was always there.
The night man, of course, was allowed a few winks when calls on his service were spare,
But nevertheless he needed more rest and tried to get it next day,
So often he arranged for the other lab men in the cupboard to hide him way.

Once he was tucked in cosy and warm, he could sleep there for hours undisturbed;
But if he were caught by a snap inspection, we'd all be sorely perturbed.
Of course we took steps to camouflage him, to hide him by stacks of supplies;
Our ruse worked quite well, not once was he seen by the probing of officer's eyes.

This was a crisis that not I alone but each of us who worked in the lab
Found we'd survive without too much sweat if at it we'd but make a stab.
Our sergeant was great at distracting inspectors, he knew ev'ry trick in the book;
We worked as a team the secret to keep of our furtive somniferous nook.

Mar. 10, 1993

A noble tree was felled to make the stuff
To house the mindless scribbles here embossed,
But now some ink upon the page conveys
At least a protest mild against the waste,
Although, perhaps, dingbats would be preferred.

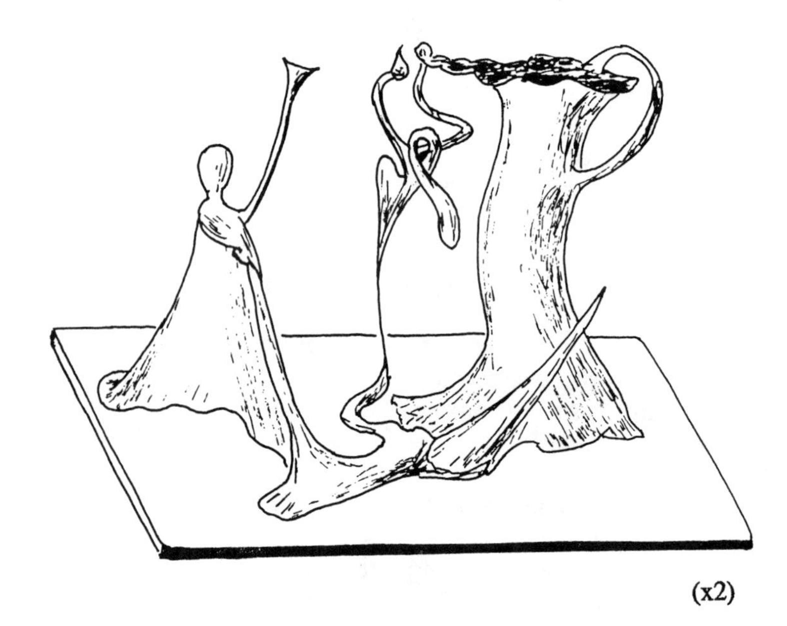

(x2)

Part THREE

CHILDHOOD

Blank verse adorns the page where once was nought.
The trick, it seems, is now to add some sense,
Some deep, revealing thought disclose and so
Imagination send in flight sublime.
But what a strain the mind to tax, and taxed,
Produce results that justify the time
And compensate the one who reads the stuff
For having labored to the end and found:
There's nothing there!

THE BATEAU

For quite a while they had dreamed of a boat, one they could call their own;
They didn't want to wait for years, wait until they were grown.
At the age of twelve they made up their minds to build themselves a boat,
Not very big, not very grand, but something at least that would float.

So they saved up their nickels and saved up their dimes, 'til two or three dollars they had;
The rest of the sum for wood and nails they got from a helpful Dad.
Then with their wagon they went into town to buy the needed supplies.
The sight of the two and the order they placed for the dealer was quite a surprise.

How their wee wagon could hold all the wood was more than he could see:
(The pieces of wood were twelve feet long, the wagon was less than three.)
With four feet or more projecting in front, the same amount out from the rear,
How could the two control such a load and still manage somehow to steer?

A rope from the tongue to the boy out in front, his pal holding tight at the back,
The dealer was amazed at the progress they made, how neatly the wagon would track.
Some twine they had tied around the planks to keep them from going askew,
So all that was left was to push and pull, it was all they had to do.

As they moved along down the village street, the merchants and passersby
Broke out a smile on ev'ry face, a twinkle in ev'ry eye.
Those who bet the load would fall before they got it home
Were sad to see not one plank try from the perilous stack to roam.

They got all the lumber safely home and stacked it on the ground
Along with all the other stuff around the house they'd found:
Paint and tar and caulking rope to finish off the task;
With hammer, saw and lots of nails, 'twas all that one could ask.

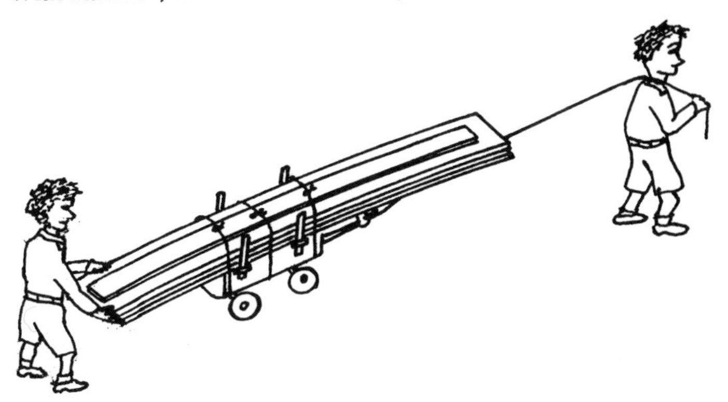

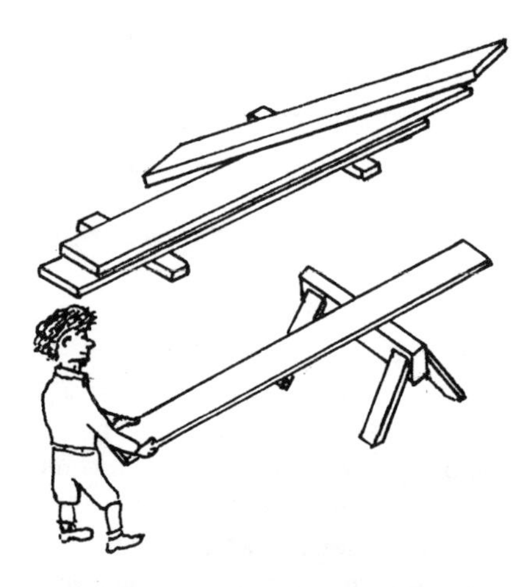

They nothing knew about building boats, though one or two they had seen,
But that would never stymie them, they both were far too keen.
They worked for days and days on end, the vessel soon took shape,
And all their friends and family, too, would stand about and gape.

When at last the job was done, the joints all tight and sound,
They filled it up with water to see what leaks were found.
With rope and tar they plugged them up, they stopped up all the leaks,
And drained the boat and let it dry for weeks and weeks and weeks.

The weeks passed by and changed to months, the months then changed to years;
They weren't allowed to launch the boat, their mothers had such fears.
The river nearby was a ruthless one, young lives it gladly took,
And that is how the two young lads sailors' lives forsook.

Feb. 6, 1993

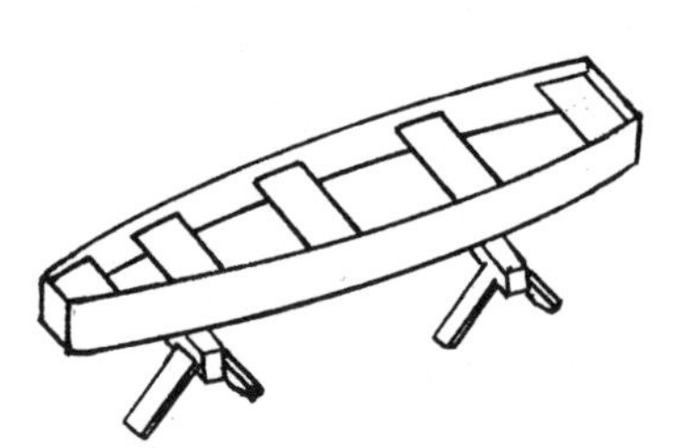

THE GREAT MINIATURE-GOLF-COURSE COMPETITION

Long years ago, before TV, when kids had lots to do,
The craze of golf in miniature spread o'er our happy land.
Grown folks liked to play at night, teenage kids did, too,
But some of us just had to watch, we had no cash in hand.

It looked like fun to those of us who were too young to play.
A few kind folks would let us in to hit the ball a bit,
But bedtime came quite early, then, we weren't allowed to stay,
And, anyhow, it wasn't fun just to watch and sit.

It wasn't long before we kids—two pals next door and I—
Frustrated by the lack of cash to play the grown-folks' game,
Decided that we'd make a course—at least we'd have a try.
We'd never even tried before, but we'd do it just the same.

Having given the matter serious thought (for about two minutes each),
We then went to our own back yards and started working hard.
Each of us seemed eager to learn and each the others to teach;
Nothing seemed to slow us down or our progress to retard.

We set our sights quite high, it seems: we'd have a dozen holes;
The sandy soil in both our yards made digging such a snap:
With little more than a sharpened stick, why, we could dig like moles.
Our course, we hoped, would bristle soon with many an ingenious trap.

But first we made a little stream that wandered all around
With water from the garden hose and dikes and dams galore.
We set a basic pattern out to use the stuff we'd found,
And if we didn't have enough, we'd simply find some more.

The stuff we found was junk, you see: tin cans and scraps of wood,
But tunnels soon and bridges, too, and traps of various kinds
We had in mind and buckled down and made as best we could;
The final product, we all knew, depended on those lucky finds.

Lovely paths for the ball we made by pushing a brick through the sand;
A rounded stone became the ball and satisfied our need.
The clubs we made would do the job, though they surely were not grand;
It all was pretty crude, I know, but it gave us joy indeed!

We'd bat those balls around the course until we almost dropped;
For us the game was just as real as the one the grown folks played.
All our other serious tasks by miniature golf were stopped,
Or if they were not really stopped, they certainly were delayed.

I wonder now if kids today who sit and watch TV
Instead of making things themselves and learning useful skills
Will have the fortitude when grown to be content as we
And manage yet somehow to cope with life and all its ills?

Feb. 9, 1993

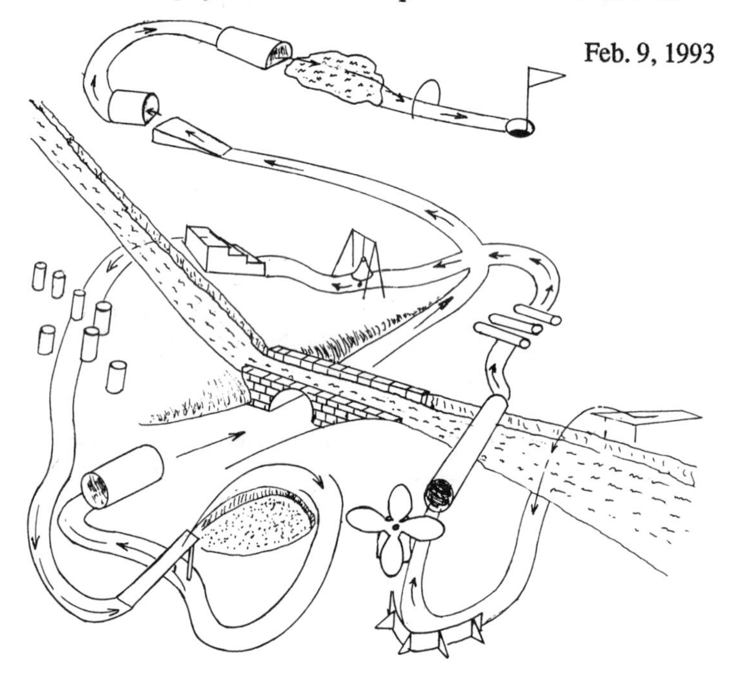

MY NARROW ESCAPE

As we go through life, we don't always know what narrow escapes we've had:
Perhaps we've missed some horrible fate for which we later are glad.
I know, for example, from my own experience, though the knowledge came quite late,
That my own professional career was changed by an event in my youthful state.

I never was good at arithmetic—my teacher knew this well—
She'd keep me in in the afternoon well past the quitting bell.
I told her that before night came I had to milk my cow,
But I suppose that still she thought that to her will I'd bow.

The plan she proposed one day to me seemed poor and quite unsound;
Indeed, I know by nature 'twas one on which my Jersey frowned;
The teacher thought she saw a way to keep me there at school,
But little did she realize it broke a natural rule.

Her plan for me was that each morn I'd start by milking twice.
She didn't know how absurd this was: an *udderly* senseless device.
I cast my lot with the cow, of course, milked her morn and night,
Which meant I couldn't stay at school and get my figures right.

The years rolled by and math remained for me a mystery,
And that is why I chose to work in natural history,
Where algebra and calculus were simply less endearing
Than when one turned one's mind to think of things like engineering.

Instead of working with figures all day and formulae galore,
My life was spent with a microscope and wee creatures that I adore.
What a narrow escape I had that day, all over milking cows!
How deliriously happy, though, one can be when one to Nature bows!

Mar. 8, 1993

THE OLD MILL STREAM AT LAKEWOOD PARK

One time a year, as a very special treat, our family went to the city.
We were only allowed to stay a few days, which seemed to us a great pity,
For while we were there we saw many things that didn't exist back home:
Concerts and theatres, the famous cyclorama, the capitol itself with its golden dome.

But the greatest thrill of all, no doubt, was the wondrous amusement park:
The merry-go-round, the Ferris wheel—a magical place after dark.
I was really too young for the roller coaster, its speed took my breath away,
But the merry-go-round and its music divine I remember quite well to this day.

Of all the rare treats we found in that park, the one that appealed most to me
Was the ride in a boat through the old mill stream, the delights of that trip to see.
We boarded the boat in a well-lit room, and the flow of the stream took charge:
Each boat only carried two or three kids, they really weren't terribly large.

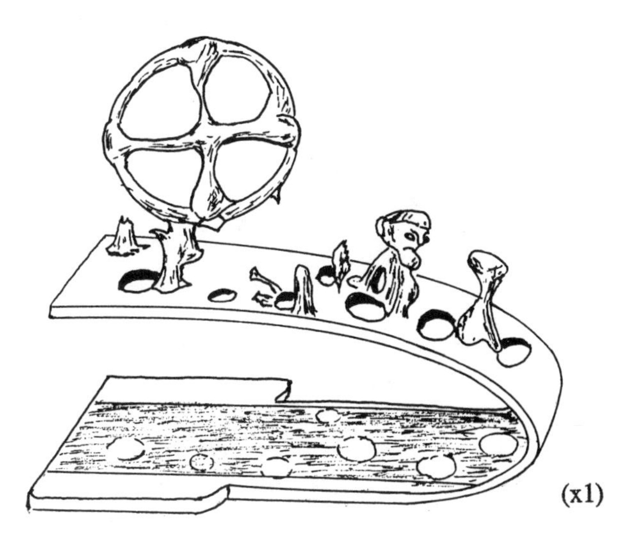

(x1)

It was delightful to drift with that free-flowing stream as it lapped on the sides of the boat;
How wondrous the mill that powered the stream and the vessel that kept us afloat!
Our time in bright light was brief, indeed; we soon saw a dark tunnel loom
And were engulfed for a while in a night pitch black, a time of terrible gloom.

But just as our fears were taking hold, a light far ahead we could see,
Mysterious to behold, it boosted our spirits; we all wondered what it could be.
As the boat swept along from the dark to the light a wonderful scene met our eyes:
We flowed with the stream into a sunlit land—oh, what a glorious surprise!

There were fields and cows and a wee tiny town, all in miniature;
The desire to see next what loomed round the bend was more than we kids could endure.
We heard the cow bells tinkling away, the bells of the church chiming, too,
And off in the distance we saw little kids, just like the ones we knew.

But all at once as we floated along, the light began to fade;
The tunnel once more the mysterious change from light to dark had made.
As we drifted along through the blackened night, we heard a donkey bray—
A flash of light, a kick and a crash—and the boat was on its way.

We rounded a bend and soon emerged just where we'd started out;
At the sight of Mom and Dad again we all let out a shout.
Oh, the joys of childhood days, the pleasures of our youth
Should fit us well for life ahead, happily seeking the Truth!

Mar. 10, 1993

REMOTE CONTROL IN THE SHUTTERED TOWER

Our home was no castle, but it did have a tower, in a sleepy American town;
The tower had windows, the windows had shutters to close when we all settled down.
The streetlight outside shone brightly upstairs, but the shutters dealt with it quite well,
But whether the shutters were open or not my mother downstairs could not tell.

When I went to bed the shutters were shut, the room was dark and dreer.
I recall, as a child, though I never knew why, that the darkness I always did fear,
So I rigged up a scheme with some nails and twine for opening the shutters from bed;
There thus was no need to get up at all and disobey what mother had said.

What a relief it always was to be able to have some light
Simply by pulling the strings I had rigged to open the shutters at night.
My ruse was no secret, it couldn't have been, my mother could see nails and strings,
Which just goes to show how a mother's real love true happiness for ev'ryone brings.

As soon as she saw that my fear of the dark was one not easy to banish,
She gave me a flashlight all of my own with which I could make darkness vanish.
A favorite game was to shine the light inside a bedclothes tent,
Although I am sure this wasn't the use my mother for it had meant.

From that time on I always had a flashlight near at hand,
Though how I came to have my first was nothing that I had planned.
My mother just saw the shutter controls, deduced the reason why,
And then concluded that a nice flashlight was what for me they'd buy.

What a rich blessing were parents like ours who loved us and did all they knew
To help us along through the rough spots in life with a love that always rang true!
As the years rolled by we always knew that by them we would be understood,
That the help and advice they so freely gave was surely for our own good.

Mar. 9, 1993

THE ROCKING-CHAIR TRAIN

The house where we lived was handsome and large, a nice bit of Victoriana,
With gables galore, a large round tower, and a lovely expansive veranda.
The memories I have of life as a youth are joyful to contemplate:
The stream of happiness in those years seemed always to flow at full spate.

Though little we had by standards of today, back then it seemed to take less
To keep us content at work and play, to give us true happiness:
A stick made a horse we could ride for hours day after day after day,
A small bag of marbles, some holes in the sand: 'twas all that one needed to play.

A brick pushed along through the sandy soil made a road lovely and wide
For a wood-block car that we'd built ourselves, our latest joy and pride.
One of the sights most thrilling to see in the dark of a summer night
Was a trolley car made from an old shoe box with windows and a candle for a light.

But the major event for a summer day when the sun was replaced by rain
Was to go to the veranda with some blankets and sheets and assemble a rocking-chair train.
The chairs were turned over, stretched in a line, the blankets dropped over them all,
Making a lovely long train with darkened cars, deep into which we could crawl.

While the rain beating down made the noise for the train, we all were safe inside;
The blanketed cars were snug and warm, a wonderful place to hide!
Many a journey we made on those days, happy in our rocking-chair train.
Where'er I go, what'er I do, its mem'ry will always remain.

Mar. 9, 1993

THE ROLLER COASTER

Little boys can be quite brave at times, I once knew two who were;
One of the two would think up a scheme, the second would bravely concur.
The second would next devise a plan and the first would give him support,
And so they progressed with plot after plot, each in his turn a good sport.

They not only had plans, this knee-panted pair; they knew how to put them to use.
Their attack was direct, their ideas were sound, with nothing about them abstruse.
They'd gather their tools, collect their supplies, and push right ahead with the chore;
Soon the idea became a goal reached, the two had succeeded once more!

The tree-house they planned was brave in concept, in execution quite grand;
The young engineers were happy with it; it worked out just as they'd planned.
Undeniable their bravery, too, in erecting a structure so high,
For to build it required both courage and skill, a fact that none can deny.

The next project, too, was designed for the brave; from the roof of the house it would run:
A small roller coaster on an oil-greased track was now what the two had begun.
They built it all up, supported it well, and saw that the sled ran true;
Test runs to make with people aboard was clearly the next thing to do.

Where did the lads, brave as they were, turn for the help they required?
I'll tell you a secret you mustn't repeat; these the events that transpired:
They conned their two sisters, younger than they, into taking the very first ride,
And they watched from the ground as the trusting young girls came roaring down the slide.

It just so happened that all went well, the contraption was safe and secure;
The faith that the sisters had in their brothers was worth what they had to endure.
Blind faith, indeed, the two girls had, but, oh, there was something more:
In fearless courage and bravery, far o'er their brothers' they'd soar.

Feb. 2, 1993

THE TURBINE ON THE BROOK

Our own yard didn't have one, but, fortunately, grandmother's did:
A lovely little natural stream, just the size for a kid.
It wasn't swift, it wasn't large—two feet across at most—
Still it was a place for dreams of which a child could boast.

We called it The Branch, and that it was—of slight concern it's name—
A jewel to use, a joy supreme, 'twill always be the same.
That stream was an ocean, a river, a sea: whatever was needed it was.
It had waves and storms and locks and dams; it even had small sand bars.

A young engineer of hydraulics I was, or a captain of a homemade ship;
One day a dam and a system of canals, another an ocean trip.
A paddle-wheel steamer with paddles that turned, powered by a stout rubber band;
I'd stand there and watch as it battled the flow, struggling away from the land.

My noblest ambition was to build a turbine like one in a book I had seen.
It turned out to be too difficult for me, its sheet-metal work was mean.
But here I am now, seventy years old; I still have the dream and the book,
And, oh, how I'd love to go home and build that turbine on the brook!

Feb. 4, 1993

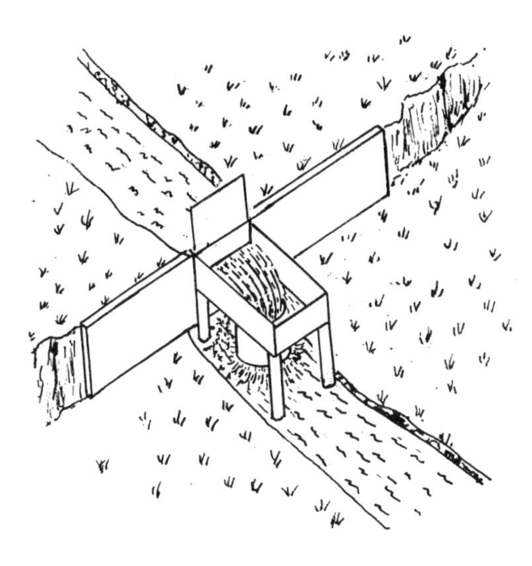

I think that I shall never see blank verse
That justifies the felling of a tree,
A tree that draws its strength from earth below
And strives to reach the lofty heights of heaven.

But then, again, the thought, perhaps, occurs
That verse, though blank, may also draw from earth
And life a strength as noble as a tree
And add a bit to make our lives attempt
To rise to heights as lofty as its own.

(x1.25)

Part FOUR

MUSIC

Blank was the *verso*, blank is the verse, and blank
Fatuity: incognitance at fault.
A void replaced by nugatory verse
Remains an innocent vacuity.

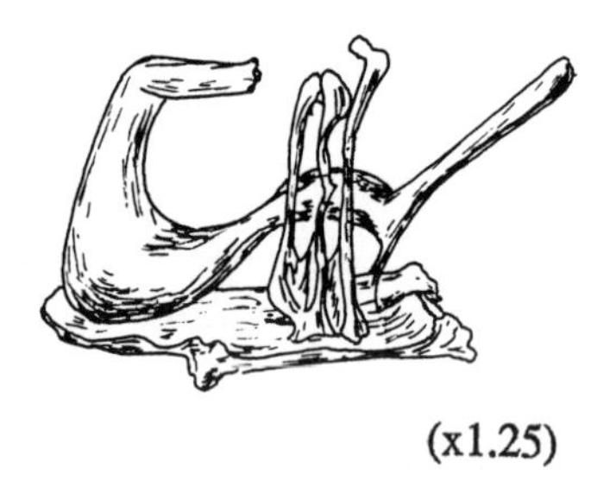

(x1.25)

THE DIRGE OF MUSIC UNHEARD

Thwarted dreams, abandoned hopes, of these life has its share,
And the way that talents are meted out so often seems unfair.
Why does one achieve his goal, acquire the skills he sought,
And yet another fall far short, his efforts come to nought?

Quite clear, sometimes, the reason is, a simple one, indeed:
One knew so hard he had to work, the other saw no need
To spend the time practicing, knuckling down each day
For an hour or two with an instrument he'd really like to play.

But often, too, the facts reveal some other force at work:
The failure might just be explained by some unplanned-for quirk.
Talent there might well have been, the will to work hard, too;
Some trick of fate might intervene and thwart what one would do.

Two girls there were who started out to learn the violin;
One grew up to play quite well and much acclaim to win.
For the other, though—sad to tell— ambition soon was spent;
The reason why came out at last: termites ate her instrument.

And then there was the teenage lad who had a dream to be
An organist of note and play with some big symphony.
A pedal organ in a shack out in a forest green,
The ingredients needed all were there for a truly idyllic scene.

But Fate stepped in with a deadly pair of forces unforeseen
To change the course, deflect the goal, prevent what might have been:
Away by the vortex of Hitler's might the musical youth was drawn,
Leaving the organ in the shack to succumb as a field-mouse pawn.

The mice enjoyed the organ felts, the bellows, too, were great,
And while the lad was overseas, they ate and ate and ate.
He never returned to the bliss in the woods, but with a wife and child went west
To pursue his studies and then to teach where the chance of success was best.

As folks grow older, their bodies, too, continue to complicate things:
Arthritis in fingers can squelch the desire to play that retirement brings;
Leaky lungs can make it tough to find the air to blow a horn,
They quash one's hopes of playing well that late in life are born.

So my advice to one and all is play and practice while you're young;
Then you're prepared if Fate one day on you ill luck has sprung.
You can change your horn for a mandolin or your trombone for a flute
Just because you lack the wind required for a heftier toot.

No need to let the dreams you've had go scuttling down the drain,
You simply use the faculties that still to you remain.
If music's in your soul, you'll find some way to bring it out:
Whispered song is just as sweet, you do not have to shout!

Just do not be content, I say, to let your music stay unheard;
To give in to some quirk of Fate is really quite absurd.
With all the range of instruments with which our world abounds,
You're sure to find that one of them for you will make sweet sounds:
Even a guitar!

Mar. 2, 1993

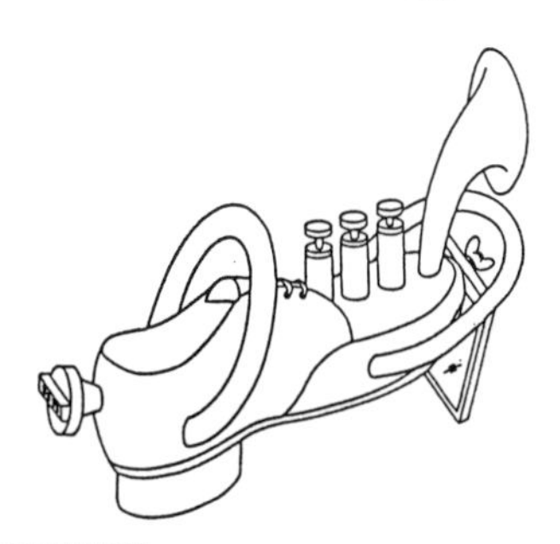

THE DREAM OF A PUNSTRUMENTEER

There are puns galore being cast aside
From the rubbish tips of the mind;
There are musical puns just hiding there
Awaiting some lucky find.

If we scrounge about through that persiflage,
We'll most certainly find what we seek:
A contorted idea, or a neat play on words,
Or a *mot* too *juste* to speak.

Badinage, I think we all will agree,
Is but a verbal rubbish pile;
It's an abstract collection of trashy bits,
But it often engenders a smile.

Isn't now the time for an ode of joy
To these two of our refuse tips:
To the wondrous collection of treasured junk
Either thrown by hand or cast by lips?

Because, once we've found a pun to distort,
Why, with suitable bits and bobs,
We can soon produce a punstrument
That's all tubes and valves and knobs.

Add a tiny harmonica—just right for the job
Of concocting a musical theme—
And our new little gadget's all ready to play,
To fulfill our comical dream.

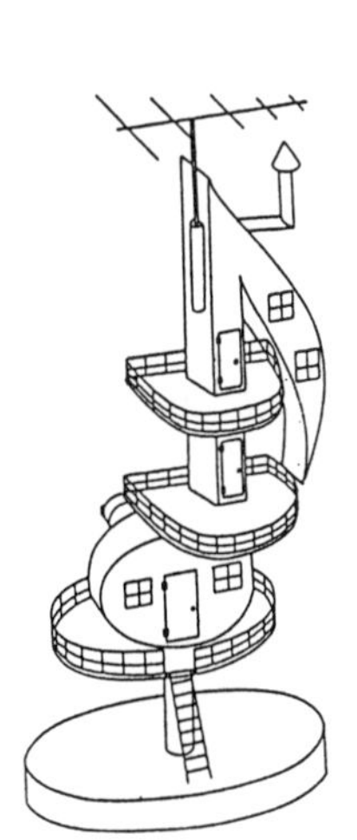

Nov. 12, 1992

First published in *Musical Punstruments* by Zach Arnold, 1994

THE MAGNIFICENT OBSESSION

How to account for obsessions folks have is a question we often might ask;
But to explain exactly how each one arose is, oh, such a delicate task!
To determine precisely when each one appeared is sometimes quite easy to do:
Folks who knew you at a very young age sometimes can furnish a clue.

At what tender age, I really don't know, a mouth organ first I did hear,
But enthrall me it did, right from the start, with melody hauntingly clear.
While quite a young lad at grandmother's knee, I picked out my first simple tune,
And so the obsession had really begun; with music I now could commune.

Piano, trombone, flute, and cornet (my parents encouraged the musical bent),
And, oh, how the peace and quiet of the day so often with music was rent.
Accordion and organ came later in life, but still the obsession remained
For the lowly harmonica, my lifelong friend, a waif by so many disdained.

If in your playing you wish to effect a change that's really dramatic,
My advice to you is simple enough: get yourself one that's chromatic.
My obsession for this began about ten and brightly it's burned ever since;
Now I suggest, though three score and ten, you're never too young to commence.

A paean today to a musical waif with a potential that's vast indeed!
The flower will bud and blossom in full if we will but plant the seed.
It's easy to carry, not heavy at all, a nice feature of such a small instrument;
The music it makes, the joy it spreads: the obsession is really magnificent!

Feb. 16, 1993

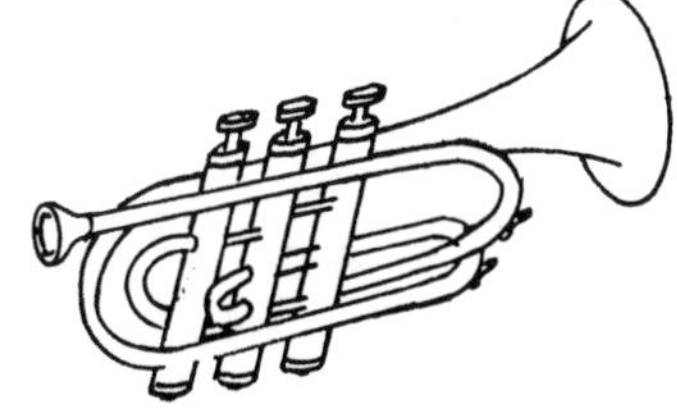

THE MUSIC MAN

He started quite young, a child in knee pants;
He'd wander about like one in a trance.
With his little harmonica he'd brighten the day,
And with a tune on his lips he'd whistle away.

While still in first grade, he the piano began
'Cause his Mum thought he'd enjoy it when he was a man.
She'd stand there beside him, hairbrush in hand
To see that he practiced, obeyed her command.

She kept at it faithfully, enforcing her belief,
'Til the seed at last sprouted and gave her relief.
But by then it was piano all day without end;
She thought it would drive her right round the bend.

His sisters had first shot at practice intense,
So the lad found his session he had to condense,
But condense it he did, enjoyed to the full,
For music on all of them had a great pull.

By twelve years of age, when his teeth were well set,
His father provided a lovely cornet.
The Methodist minister taught him to play,
For which he is grateful down to this day.

The cornet was useful, the piano was, too,
In church they both gave him a job he must do.
At college for four years, where science he had found,
His knowledge increased, but his music lost ground.

And then came the army, 'twas wartime you know,
But cornet and harmonica also could go.
The cornet was used to wake up the troops,
He'd play the harmonica to much smaller groups.

After the war, came more academe;
For thirty long years 'twas life's main theme,
When suddenly he had an attack coronary,
Which let him again make music primary.

In earlier days a flute and trombone
He started to play to vary the tone.
Three score and ten, he still could aspire
An electronic organ at last to acquire.

To compose his own tunes and write them out fine,
He'd labor for hours on each little line.
His musical notebooks continued to grow,
For melodies pursued him where'er he would go.

The Salvation Army then gave him a chance
His musical knowledge and skill to enhance.
He'd play in the band with cornet aglow,
'Til poor circulation ambition laid low.

So back to the piano, he'd play for the choir,
And thus he'd assuage a heartfelt desire.
For the army, an organist he hoped to become
By practicing hard on the one at his home.

At times, with a group of his musical friends,
He'd apply his skills to different ends.
In nursing homes, to folks at rest,
With his accordion he'd give of his best.

As life wore on, though tattered and torn,
He never was lonely and never forlorn.
With music he always could brighten the day
And help those about him chase sadness away.

Dec. 25, 1992

THE MYSTERY OF MASTERY

The mystery of mastery is practice, it seems,
Though it's something left out of our rosier dreams.
We all would develop a masterful touch
And do so quite fast, without working too much.

My Mum knew the secret, held in her hand:
A hairbrush to see that I did as she planned.
I'd practice my scales as she stood by my side,
And thus I partook of her musical pride.

But, oh, what a blessing, a mother like that,
Who loved me enough to see that I sat,
Worked on the piano and learned to play well,
Mastered the mystery, succumbed to its spell!

The lesson I learned from my Mom as a youth
Has proved to be an invaluable truth.
'Twas one to apply as I faced ev'ry task:
Just work with commitment, what more could one ask?

Study, work, devotion it takes;
Practice, practice, perfection that makes.
In learning a language, perfecting a skill,
The secret is work, self-discipline still.

If you wish to succeed, to do something well,
This is the way I've found to excell:
Just set your mind firmly to master the chore,
Then work hard and practice, and practice some more.

Jan. 24, 1993

THE ORGANIC WAY OF LIFE

One of the fondest memories I have, as a high school lad in my teens,
Is of the time that I spent alone in the woods, with all of the bliss that that means.
My Dad paid a man to build me a shack, not far from a lovely wee brook,
Where I could escape the noise of the town with an organ, some music, and a book.

The organ was the kind that you pedal to pump, its reeds a delight to the ear:
How grand to be able to play a concert that only the birds could hear,
And, oh, what a pleasure to roam through the woods and sit by that gentle stream,
Far from the hustle and bustle of life, out where one's soul could dream!

The organ was one from my grandfather's store, and, oh, it was handsome indeed!
It was made for the parlour and had shelves and drawers to store all the things one might need.
My love for the organ began in that shack as I pedalled away in the woods,
But the next fifty years were organless ones, encumbered by life's other goods.

The schism began when to college I went in a city some distance away,
And the field mice decided the organ, indeed, was something that they, too, could play.
They loved it so much they ate all the felt and ev'rything else but the wood;
Then they proceeded to fill it with young to do all the damage they could.

The army came next and years overseas, a mansion replaced the old shack;
A wife and two kids and a job way out west, to my home I'd never go back.
The organless years continued to mount, 'til I was three score and ten,
When suddenly one day, by a true quirk of fate, I had an organ again.

Those years in between on music weren't lost: the piano was practiced a lot:
Hours of work were also put in on a piano accordion I'd got,
So, nimble the fingers were kept all that time, well primed by keyboard skills,
And now in retirement I freely confess the hours that practicing fills.

But what of the organ so newly acquired, how does it compare with the old?
The progress there's been in making such things has yielded improvements untold:
A fine instrument, an electronic one, with a two-octave pedal board.
Organic ambitions now rose to the fore unfettered, indeed; now they soared!

For many long years I've struggled to play Bach's fugues and toccatas so grand
On accordion and piano—a delightful task—but Bach for the organ them planned.
Now with an organ I start out afresh to tackle its own repertoire.
How thrilling, indeed, our lives can be; how wondrous the challenges are!

Feb. 25, 1993

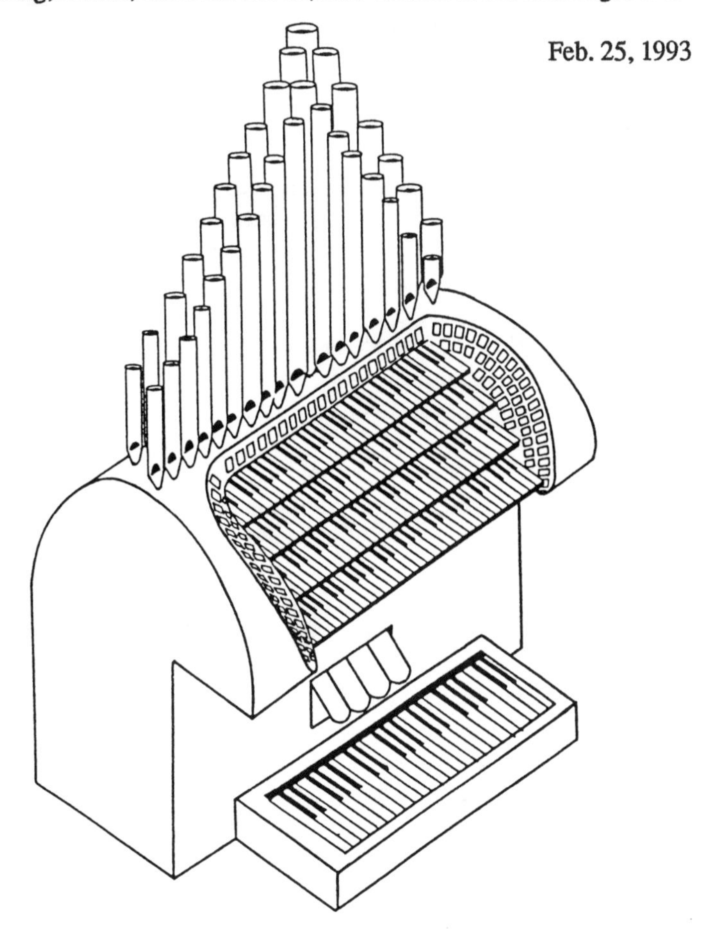

THE SONG OF THE WAYWARD HARMONICA

(Homage to Robert W. Service and *The Song of the Mouth Organ*)

Any harmonicist worth his salt needs several harmonicas to play:
One for each key he intends to use in the program he expects for the day.
They all must be chromatic, of course, if he hopes to keep up with the band;
This way he can play any note that's required and the total effect is quite grand.

In olden times they were cheap to buy, ten or twelve dollars apiece,
But that was before inflation took charge and made all the prices increase.
Now a hundred dollars almost you'll find you'll pay for each one,
But once you've acquired the ones that you need, you surely are set for some fun.

The music that's played by the band we have, rich in horns and strings,
Becomes a delight for all to hear when one of our vocalists sings.
We've six or seven of these in our troupe, a particular style for each;
Women and men, they've all learned well the lessons instructors could teach.

But where in such a respectable group can harmonicas justly fit in?
Some of the ways may surprise you indeed; to list them I now shall begin.
With a range of three octaves—chromatic ones, too—its scope is massive indeed;
It's timbre can range from mellow to thin, responding with grace to each need.

Obbligatos it takes in leaps and bounds, arpeggios are nothing at all;
Trills a delight, gruppettos a breeze, tremolos really a ball.
With such a potential for varied effect—if used with skill and grace—
It's easy to fit such an instrument in, easy to find it a place.

Among my harmonicas is one very old, for long it has served me quite well,
But one of its reeds is now out of tune, its dissonance easy to tell.
Its tonal delinquence is painful to hear unless it is used with finesse
In blues and such things where ordinary rules on occasion one can transgress.

A froward harmonica, none can deny, most frequently soweth strife,
But at times when the band, for comical effect, with intentional discord is rife,
Such willful dissent on the instrument, with its obstinacy perverse,
Adds to it all an off-key note, an effect that couldn't be worse.

Sweet indeed, though not often said, are the uses of perversity,
But do not confuse—it's easy to do—discord with artful diversity.
A chromatic harmonica with one bum reed admittedly may have its uses,
But one must be careful and skillful, indeed, to avoid its many abuses.

April 17, 1993

PART FOUR

THE BANAUSIC SIDE

The blanker the verse, the worse the case for the bilge,
The stuff that covers the page, the curse prolix
That moves us on to write still more about
Still less than what we started with, and yet,
Come out where in we went and always were
Content to dream of more and more of nought.

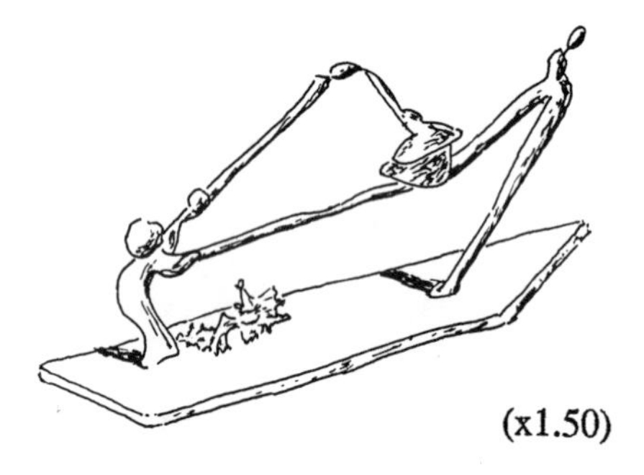

(x1.50)

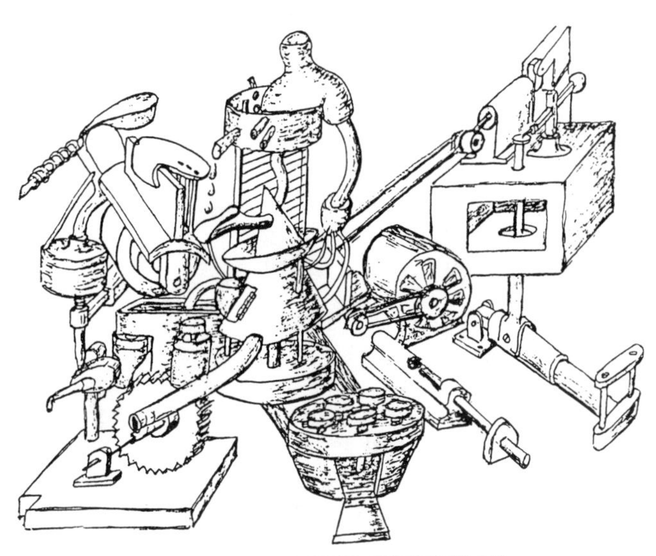

THE AMATEUR INVENTOR

The amateur inventor in his home workshop today
Reminds me of the alchemist in olden times at play.
Both of them withdrew a bit from the world as it really is
To seek some brilliant answer to a self-inflicted quiz:

How to turn base metals into truly precious gold,
Or how to make a drink to take to stop one getting old?
Some of them explored the ways of wiping out disease,
A problem, they all found, their wits did sorely tease.

Today the gadgeteer, in his workshop tucked away,
Tries with modern magic tricks some problem to allay,
But since he's not a professional and basic knowledge lacks,
His efforts often take him out on blind and fruitless tacks.

Like olden-day alchemists, who often did not know
Some basic contradictions on the path they wished to go,
The modern amateur may well attempt to use
A technique or a practice that will baffle and confuse.

A smattering of information is often all he knows,
And this can be a source for him of disappointing woes
That seldom quench the zeal of those who have true dedication
Or thwart for long the plans of those with real determination.

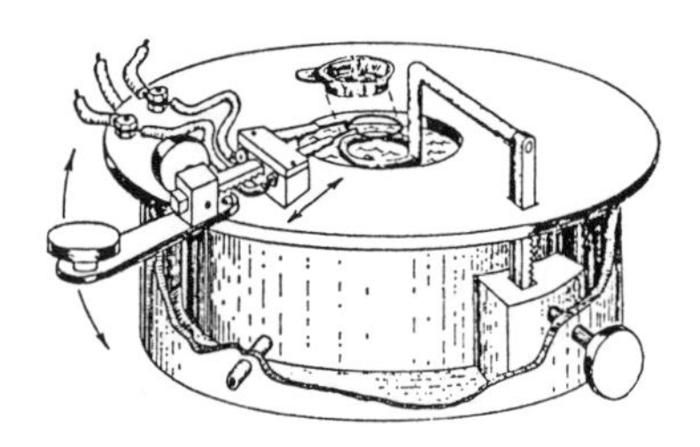

Like alchemists of long ago, many amateurs today,
Driven by the love of gold, forget their work is really play.
So they change it to a tedious chore that robs it of its greatest joy
And makes them forfeit what could be for them a priceless toy.

To go into one's shop at night, forget one's routine work,
Allows a chap to set aside those business woes that irk
And buckle down with hands and tools to try ideas he's cherished long,
To build the gear he needs to sort the right from wrong.

Perhaps he works for many nights, perhaps for just a few
Before he tumbles to the path of something really new.
But never mind how long it takes, he's learning all the while,
Perhaps creating lovely things that help make others smile.

Perhaps he'll never find a way to turn shop time to gold,
But the joy he finds as he tinkers there, sees his plans unfold,
Brings priceless good to his peace of mind, to a spirit worn by care:
Worth more to him, indeed, than gold, the simple pleasures there.

Mar.15, 1993

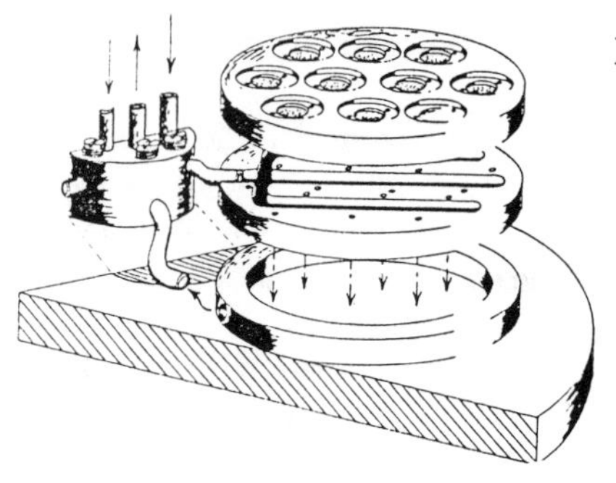

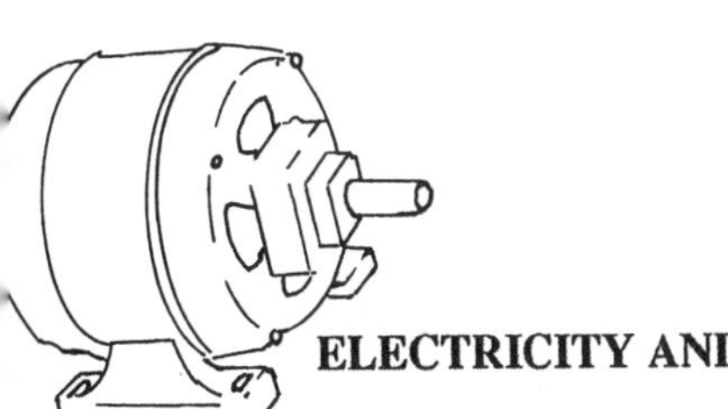

ELECTRICITY AND I DOWN THROUGH THE YEARS

Since quite a young lad I've had a friendship, uneasy though it be,
With a natural force I hold in awe: it's just electricity.
I suppose the romance began in knee pants, as I played with my electric train;
I little suspected that throughout my life respect for the stuff would remain.

Before very long a quarter-horse motor I somehow managed to acquire;
I think that it came from a washing machine that was old enough to retire.
This motor became my pride and my joy, a constant source of delight:
What a challenge it was to put it to use and learn how to harness its might!

The first thing I made— how well I recall—was a machine for polishing shoes;
With it my Dad I really could please, and shine any pair he might choose.
Next I required a circular saw, but the skill to make one I lacked;
'Twas many a year before I could launch on this a succesful attack.

Electricity is magic to me, though unschooled in its use I've remained;
I've blown lots of fuses and had some rude shocks, but a love for it I've retained.
Down through the years it's served me quite well, a long list of gadgets I've made;
With electric devices of various sorts and various designs I have played.

An untutored youth with them I remain, though now I am three score and ten;
Each time I make a connection, an adventure is soon to begin.
For me it remains a mystical force and one that I never shall know;
My ignorance of it I sincerely regret and deepest respect for it show.

As I look through the years at the things I have done with this awesome natural force,
I freely admit that for me it has been a wondrous and valued resource,
Which all goes to show that friendships can be, though shaky and not understood,
Far more productive and faithful, indeed, than ever we thought that they could.

Feb. 23, 1993

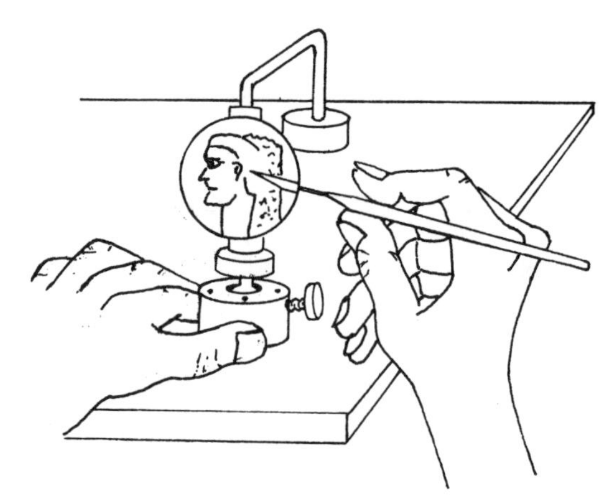

THE MINIATURIST

Bulging is our planet with this awesome human race;
All are multiplying, but there really isn't space.
By each producing fewer and always thinking small,
I think we'd soon discover there is really room for all.

Miniaturization is a fetish dear to some:
Make it ever smaller, but there's smaller still to come.
Brobdingnag was monstrous, Lilliput divine;
Surely it is better that expansion be confined.

If we carve a figure as massive as our own,
Seeds for further crowding are merely all we've sown.
But by making tiny ones, six in either hand,
We now have created something really grand.

Microcosmic pieces, yes, are easy to produce:
Whet imagination, laugh, and turn it loose.
Watch the tiny forms emerge, fine in each detail;
To captivate its audience, it surely cannot fail.

When we shall have made at last beauty that is sound,
It's easy then to make it fit some tiny space we've found.
True, we have contributed, but it's really just a little:
A jot is all we've added, or maybe just a tittle.

Dec. 18, 1992

THE MODELLER'S DREAM

There are men who are men, there are men who are not,
There are men but children bold
Who will never give up their childish ways,
Grow up just because they are old.

They remember the joy, the youthful delight,
Of a leaf that for them was a ship,
And the rain and a puddle as wide as the sea,
A wonderful place for a trip!

Then, a board for a hull and a rag for a sail,
They launched a galleon proud,
With a captain bold, an imaginary one,
And a sailor on ev'ry shroud.

O, the years passed on and the trials of life
Bent their backs and greyed their hair,
But return they would to the dreams of youth:
To the rain and the puddle and the ship so fair.

So, let's bring out the tools, spread out the plans,
We'll use all the skills we've acquired
And build a ship—an elegant one—
Expressing the dreams we have sired.

But, of course, it's still an illusion, you see,
Like the one of our youth long ago:
Our ship is only a miniature one,
But it's right that this should be so,

For the dreams of life begin in small scale,
When we ourselves are miniatures,
But they set the stage for the pageant of life,
Are, in effect, overtures.

Dreams aren't confined to the young alone;
You can have them at any age.
They just get richer and fuller with time
And nobler at ev'ry stage.

We all should take time to dream a little;
It helps to brighten the day,
And the model we make of our ship or our lives
Another may help on life's way.

But modelling, they say (the cynical ones),
Is part of a world of dreams:
Real life takes place on a far grander scale,
Where all is just what it seems;

Where ev'rything is as large as life,
Or better at twice the size;
Where fiction we make to edify strife,
A tissue erected on lies!

But don't we ourselves always remain
Miniature parts of a far grander scheme?
Aren't we just models of an imperfect sort
In a celestial modeller's dream?

Nov. 16, 1993

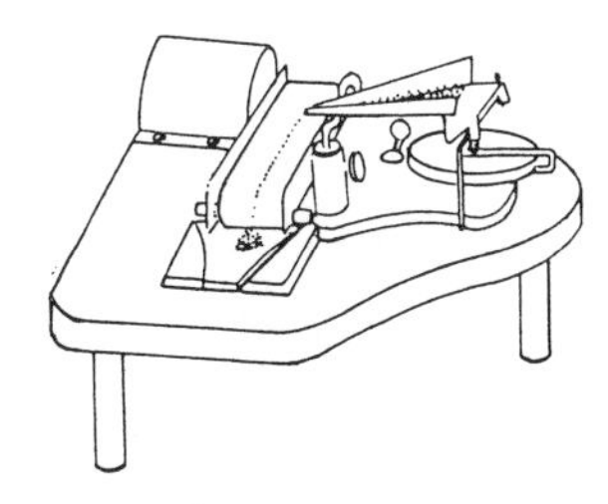

AN ODE TO BRICOLAGE

Many roam far with grants of gold
And buy most lavish gear,
All blinking lights and shiny knobs
And inner works so dear.

Why work to soil your untried hands,
When others will do so instead?
A couple of forms, some well-placed praise,
And funds galore you're fed.

Why work, indeed, in dirt and grime,
'Mid scraps and waste and treasured junk?
Why ever try to make it yourself,
In a world on subsidy drunk?

Perhaps it's pride, perhaps it's need,
Perhaps it's just plain dumb,
But to go it alone and capture success
Is a praiseworthy rule of thumb.

Oh, the nights were long and the problem tough,
And the midnight oil burned low,
But all at once a cry rang out:
"I think I stole the show".

So, where'er you go, what'er you do,
If you do it yourself you'll know,
With great satisfaction, that solitary action
Both praise and blame will bestow.

Oct. 29, 1992

First published in *A Technical Manual for the Biologist* by Zach M. Arnold, 1993

THE PASSING OF A NOBLE WAY OF LIFE

One of the noblest contrivances of man
Was the institutional garbage can.
A place where happy scavengers met
And often a pleasant surprise would get.

Many a happy morn began,
With a stop at the lowly garbage can
While earning my own Ph.D.
"Twas better by far than a grant for me,

For from the can I often fished
Bits to make some gear I wished
To assemble in my lab
When I hadn't funds to meet the tab.

A bit of brass, perhaps some wood,
Or just some string that still was good.
You never knew just what you'd find
To help a project you had in mind.

I kept a box of scrap I'd found,
A thing on which my colleagues frowned,
But in the shop these bits and bobs
Soon helped me finish lots of jobs.

I got along without the grants
That are so often won by chance.
A trip or two to the garbage bin,
And soon construction could begin.

For all the gear I made that way
A heavy price I'd have had to pay,
But the early morning scavenge hunt
Often absorbed this financial brunt.

As the years rolled by and my rank increased,
One of the habits I'd not released
Was my morning stop by the garbage can:
I still belonged to the scavenging clan.

But, as so often seems our fate,
Progress comes in deadly spate
To sweep away some youthful bliss,
Some habit dear we'll sorely miss.

Large plastic bags to seal our waste
I find offensive to my taste:
They make it tough to scrounge around
Where treasured junk is often found.

But of all of man's abominations,
Of all his adverse perpetrations,
The massive dumpster takes the cake;
My heart at sight of them doth ache.

No more can one just lift a lid
And see what in the can is hid.
No more can one just probe about
And easily pull a treasure out.

Now you need a ladder tall
To see into the beast at all.
No longer can the amateur
The rigours of modern technology endure.

The age of dumpsters is not for me,
The truth of this is plain to see.
I'll step aside with one desire:
Take my junk, go home, retire.

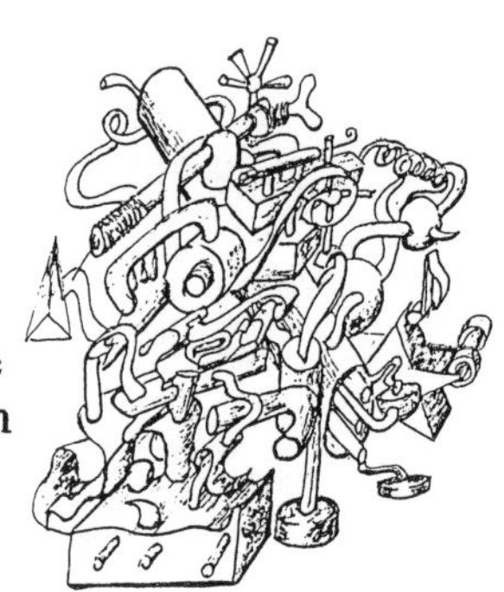

Now in my little shop at home
The junk and I are free to roam
Down paths of creativity,
Not victims of passivity!

Each day presents some challenge new.
The junk and I know just what to do
To make a new piece of biological gear
And meet the need of the gadgeteer.

My junk-gathering years pay rich dividends
And thwart the dumpsters and other new trends,
For here at home, with far less stress,
Postponed problems I now can address.

The bits and pieces I salvaged with care
Are often adapted—with little to spare—
In assembling a tool for research underway
And help achieve the goal for the day.

So I'll never regret those early morn trips
To the university garbage tips;
And the problem of dumpster penetration
I gladly bequeath to a new generation.

Sept. 8, 1993

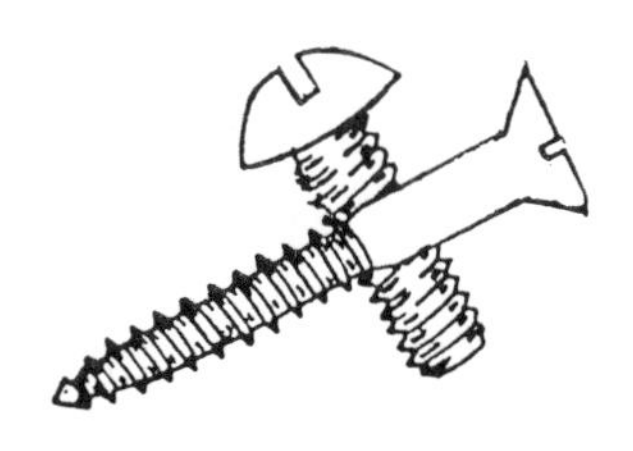

A TALE OF TWO FASTENERS

This is a story I've long wished to tell,
Though 'twill never make headline news.
It's about a couple I've long known well,
A pair of simple screws.

One was a screw for working with wood,
The other for use on machines;
Each did its job as well as it could,
Each applied fully its means.

They started together in the place they were made,
But soon were sent their separate ways:
One to the country, for years there it stayed,
One to the city to start off its days.

The wood screw was country and well might it be,
With trees grown for timber and wood all about.
A city the screw for machines was to see,
And was happier to be there, no doubt.

The wood screw was bought by a young country lad.
A table for drafting it helped him to build,
The proudest possession the young fellow had,
An early ambition with it was fulfilled.

The same lad at college once needed a screw;
He found what he needed on a trip to the town
To make a machine for research he must do,
And that's how the pal for the wood screw was found.

He early determined that after each use
He'd salvage those screws for the next job at hand.
He'd use them with care, avoiding abuse,
Give both of them lives that were noble and grand.

Each was kept busy down through the years
With assignments both crude and refined.
Each struggled nobly to outdo its peers
And never a project declined.

A long list of tasks the wood screw has done,
At home or at work, in lab or in shop:
Bunks for the kids, a place for each one,
With one down below, the other on top.

A fume hood, a field desk, and a typewriter stand,
But later all were revamped.
The screw wound up in a new project, planned
To relieve some space that was cramped.

His pal, the machine screw, was quite busy too;
He hadn't a moment's reprieve.
He always was given some new job to do;
His full range of tasks is hard to believe:

A grinder for fossils, a small microtome,
A gadget to test tasting in flies,
A plastics extruder for the workshop at home,
A viewer to help aging eyes.

So each screw was busy throughout his career,
With dignity each of them served.
Each played its role, valued and dear,
From duty each never swerved.

Don't they deserve a plaque of some sort,
To honor such service sincere?
They worked and they slaved without a retort,
At least without one I could hear.

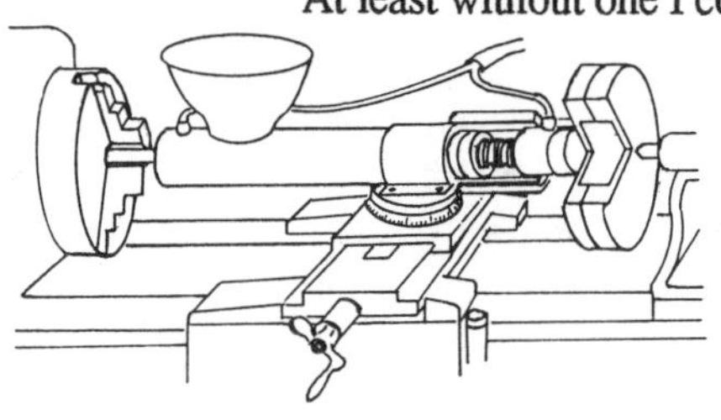

So I'll pay them credit with this little rhyme;
'Tis I they have served so well.
I'm grateful indeed for their work and their time,
I'm honored their story to tell.

But a postlude now hear to the tale we've told,
A happy event for the two:
Just as they both are growing old,
They are finally united in the task they must do.

For years they had gone their separate ways,
But they yearned to work as a pair.
Now, at last, they can end their days
In a common task they can share.

A computer has come to live with us;
We used them both in its installation.
Each plays its role without any fuss;
To see them thus is real inspiration.

Now happy they are, at last united,
Associates in a task.
Parted years are now requited,
Nought more of life do they ask.

Jan. 27, 1993

WHAT CLASS YOUR FARE?

All aboard the train of life, departure time is nigh!
Choose your class and settle down, but do not aim too high.
If you choose a space too fancy or one that's too refined,
Nothing there but discontent is what you'll likely find.

Travelling only first class, where *I* is number one,
There's seldom heartfelt laughter and little kindness done:
Just comfort for oneself, security and peace;
Care, concern for others, from these we buy release.

But step along the corridor to the realms of lower class;
Here it isn't easy just to sit and watch life pass.
Here we are a part of it, partaking to the full,
Share its joy and sorrow, know compassion's pull.

Join the mirth and laughter, share your picnic lunch,
Play your tin harmonica, brighten up the bunch.
Lend a caring hand to a heart in deep distress,
Help to lift a spirit through some act of kindliness.

This train is not for one alone: its here for all of us;
How quickly we appreciate its clutter and its muss,
For this way leads to happiness, fulfillment most sublime,
By far the best investment of our fleeting earthly time.

Dec. 18, 1992

PART SIX

A MUSING GRACE

There once was is a land not far away,
Quite easy to achieve by simple flight
Of fancy or imagination bold,
By all who care to make the trip alone
And aren't afraid of what the neighbors say;
An optomisty rhapsodaisical land
Where stars lament the hue of blissful eve.
Trisandral charge—halloo, hallay, halas!—
Stops few who have the time to sit and dream.
Archiambocymphlometric haste
Is still no match for drifting with the tide,
Nor can it slake the silence of the night.

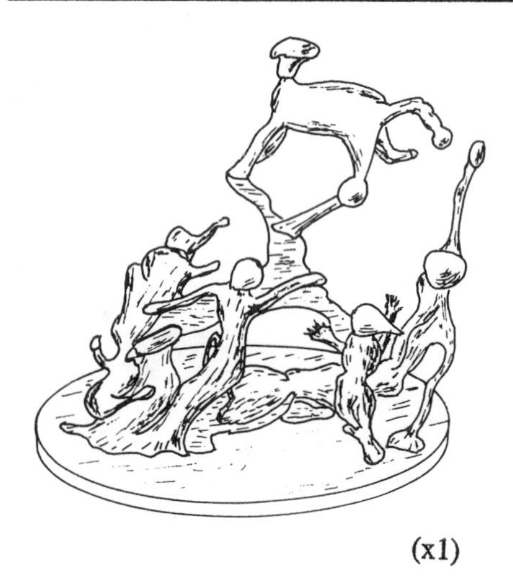

(x1)

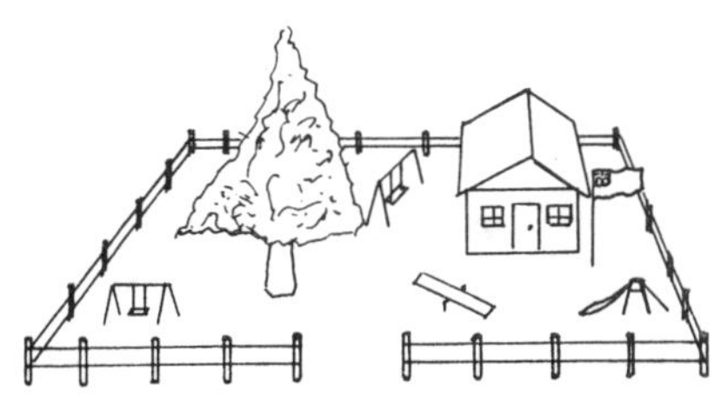

THE CLASS REUNION

Oh, how I wish I could have gone back home again this year
To see once more my classmates there, the ones who are so dear.
I haven't been for years and years, the strain is now too great,
But lovely memories of them all I still appreciate.

I remember childhood days, the things we used to do,
The old folks and the young, the places that we knew,
Our family home, the toys we had, the games we used to play,
The lessons and the homework too, the chores that came each day.

I remember best of all my Mom and Dad and sisters three.
The six of us had many a year as happy as could be,
But then in time we kids grew up and went our separate ways,
To live our lives as best we could and make worthwhile our days.

Our classmates, too, are scattered wide, though some have stayed near home;
A lot of us have been abroad, the army helped us roam,
But after years of faithful toil, we try for home again
To see our pals just one time more, unless it's too much strain.

From three score years to three score ten, we all are getting on;
Each year our numbers seem to shrink: some more of us are gone.
When health makes travelling seem unwise, the telephone, though, is good
For swapping news, exchanging views with all the friends we should.

And then, of course, through letters, too, with them you can commune,
'Specially with the ones with whom you seem to be in tune.
So do not fret if you just can't go to be with the gang that day;
If you really wish to keep in touch, there surely is a way.

Pick up the nearest telephone or just a ball-point pen;
It takes so little time to call or fit a letter in.
Each call you make, each time you write, you share with some old friends
Memories of days gone by and a love that never ends.

Feb. 14, 1993

THE FACTS OF LIFE

Some of the facts of life are ever so easy to prove,
The proof so abundant 'round us, to see it we needn't move.
The sun, for example, rises and starts off on its daytime show
Just 'cause some wakeful cockerel thought its was time he should crow.

Another such fact is not too well known, though its proof is equally clear:
It has to do with the spirits of the dead, of those to us that are dear.
The reason, of course, the truth is obscure and not so generally known
Is that spirits are black not white, as they usually for us are shown.

Spirits are shy of light in all forms; whenever they see it they flee,
And that, I suspect, is the reason why they sometimes aren't easy to see.
But spirits *en masse* are easy to see if you but know where they are:
When grouped all together, they're one black blob, blacker than asphalt tar.

To prove this fact, just close your eyes and see ev'rything go black;
With light expelled the spirits have returned, *en masse* they've come rushing back.
And all that you see with your eyes tightly shut is the mass of that deep black throng.
When someone proclaims that spirits aren't seen, you know right off they are wrong.

But if they say "That isn't enough, for what you see with your eyes, indeed,
Is just not the proof that's required; in fact, the proof that we need
Should be seen by all and all at once, an experience easily shared."
The facts are not altered a bit by that charge, and this bold appeal is now dared:

To see such real proof, just gather your friends on a night without moon or stars;
The spirits are there, massed as before, black as the night they are.
All can there see the black spirit mass, convinced that it's all very real.
Those are the facts, quite easy to see, on which is based this bold appeal.

Jan. 28, 1993

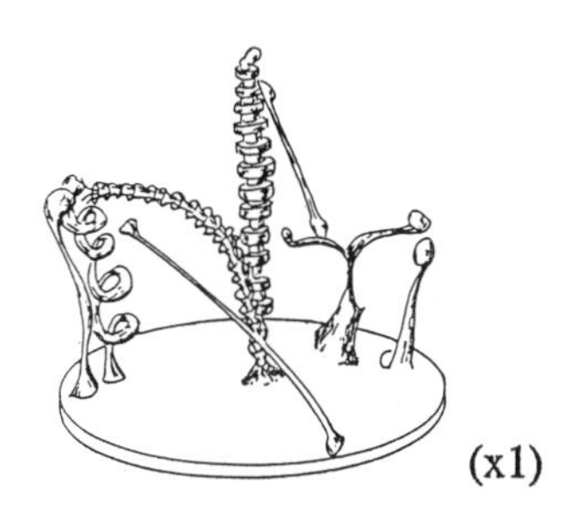

(x1)

FASCINATING IRRELEVANCIES

Fascinating irrelevancies: we see them ev'ry day;
They seem to be so popular, perhaps they're here to stay.
We all receive our share of them and wonder what they mean;
By some we're left unscathed, by others caught between.

Some deflect us from our course, disrupt our pleasant dreams;
Another makes us wonder if it's ev'rything it seems.
This unexpected turn of things let's put to good account:
Some problem that is troubling us, perhaps we'll then surmount.

Fascinating, yes, that indeed; irrelevant too, no doubt,
But there's more than meets the naked eye, as we'll likely soon find out.
They can stimulate our interest, slow our hectic pace,
Help combat depression, save us from disgrace.

Broadening their influence, revealing their effect,
And the change they bring about is easy to detect.
They help our understanding, enrich our daily life,
Help us battle boredom, sooth internal strife.

They add both zest and humour along life's weary way,
Renew and feed the spirit, help blow cares away.
Puns and lowly punstruments, typical of the breed,
Are here for our improvement, I hope you will concede.

Synoptic vision they encourage, perspective help adjust,
Help develop values one can really trust.
Aids to sublimation, pomposity deflate,
Soul-food, inspiration all appreciate.

Fascinating irrelevancies: we all should sing their praise.
They lighten up life's journey and brighten up our days.
Where'd we be without the pleasures they can sow?
If, of course, you don't know now, I fear you'll never know.

Jan. 19,1993

THE FRENZIED SEARCH FOR THE LOST NIGHTCAP

A warm nightcap is a blissful thing
When cold night air's about.
To wear one helps true warmth to bring
When the household heat is out.

One morning when from sleep I arose,
I could not find my cap.
Numb my hands, and cold my nose:
A really frigid chap!

I knew the loss of temperature
Was due to loss of cap,
But where I found that cap, for sure,
Made me feel a sap.

Both high and low I'd looked for it,
Beneath the bed, just ev'rywhere:
In any place it might have lit.
Alas, alack, it was not there.

And then at last, as I quit the sack
And changed from nightclothes into day,
The cap fell down from off my back
And at my feet there lay.

It seems that in the night, some way
It worked into my sleep attire,
And that is where it came to stay
To cause disruptions dire.

Dec. 29, 1992

FRIENDS THROUGH THE FENCE

One is a boy, the other a dog; how lovely their friendship to see!
The love that they have, the devotion they show, is a sterling example for you and me.
Though a seven-foot fence is erected between, this their ardor cannot suppress;
Each standing there on his side of the fence has found the secret of true happiness.

Each morning we watch them from our windows above as they gather to commune at the fence.
This is the way they always prefer to have their morning commence:
The boy dressed for school, the dog just awake, each one awaiting his friend.
A cry of delight from each rends the air, the night's separation at last at an end.

We see the two there, each on his side, dog licking boy through the wire,
Or each one just sitting, looking at the other, neither of them seeming to tire.
Damon and Pythias would have been proud to call these two disciples of theirs,
For the heritage of friendship the Sicilians passed on, these two are indeed worthy heirs.

Each, I've no doubt, would risk his own life—not give it a second thought—
If by such a deed of self sacrifice the life of his friend could be bought.
But, happily for us in this day and age, such heroics should not be required;
Still, the example set by these two is something that's greatly admired.

May 3, 1993

GIFTS

To some is given the gift of gab:
The words flow out in torrents.
There's nought in their speech that's drab,
And nought to cause abhorence.

To some are given ideas grand
To help reshape man's fate,
But most receive far less than planned
And do things far less great.

No matter how the ideas come
Or just what form they take:
They all add up to quite a sum
And give you quite a stake.

The trick, I've found, is to write them down,
So they become your own.
They'll never help you gain renown
If from your head they've flown.

You never know when one might come,
So be prepared to jot it down:
Perhaps it's trite or seems to be,
But written down it's there to see.

The gift might be a flowing line
Of words or music clear;
Just write it down: it might be fine
And soon become quite dear.
(To you, at least.)

Out of the blue these gifts descend;
Whence or why they come, who knows?
Perhaps above some kindly friend
On us below the gift bestows.

But with the gift there comes the task
Of putting it all to use:
You cannot in its glory bask
If it remains abstruse.

You'll have to work to develop it,
To make it prove worthwhile;
You mustn't be content to sit
And let the thought beguile.

But put to use, developed well,
The gift idea will blossom out.
Perhaps at first it's hard to tell
Just what it's all about,

But when you once gain mastery
And bend it to your will,
You'll find it's hidden mystery
Becomes much clearer still.

And when at last it's all your own
To give to ev'ry one,
You'll know, from the little seed you've sown,
A worthwhile deed you've done.

Feb. 19, 1993

MEMOIRES

Many write memoires on which they can gloat
(They often have much to be said),
But I've done so little that's worthy of note,
I've attempted to put it in verse instead.

Ever since finding my health on the skids,
I should have been plagued by a nameless dread
Of leaving no record behind for the kids
By keeping it locked in my head.

But, I'm afraid, it's simply not so:
The longer I live, the happier I get,
Knowing that when it is my time to go,
At least I have battled the problems I've met.

My life has been simple, no cause to boast,
But I find it such fun to try to write verse,
I have to jot down what's pleased me the most
Before they extract me from here in a hearse.

Oct. 27, 1993

MY ENGLISH PRIZES

Oh, yes, tweed jackets: I have at least four;
Of wool English sweaters I have even more.
Some real English tools you'll find in my shop;
I've a journal subscription they never let stop.

All of these things and quite a few more
I found as a soldier abroad on that shore.
But found above all, all else in my life,
Is a pal from there: A real English wife.

My English piano is my other real prize;
It's cost was quite modest, but so is its size.
I often compare them, the piano and wife:
Each is a cure for tension and strife.

For years I have striven to master the two,
Done ev'rything that I knew to do.
With the piano, I feel that some progress I've made,
But I've still much to learn from that dear English maid.

The keys and the strings of the piano are worn,
And I myself am now tattered and torn,
But my wife is still steadfast and never complains,
Thoughtful and caring she always remains.

With the piano it's easy discords to make;
Sometimes I make them for their own sake,
But marital discord my dear wife abhors.
I know quite well what she adores:

Harmony, true and clear to the end;
She always is striving discord to mend.
While I on the piano sweet melodies find,
She creates beauty of a far nobler kind.

And so we three live our lives here together.
For fifty grand years we've managed to weather
The slings and arrows of outrageous Fate,
My piano, and I, and my wonderful mate.

Feb. 20, 1993

MY FIRST FORAM

High above the water's edge,
Well up the river bluff,
Protrudes a hard resistant ledge
That's filled with fossil stuff.

The beds in age are not so old,
Their life was of the sea.
Though some prefer to search for gold,
It's fossil shells for me.

The river was a murd'rous one,
Two lives it claimed one year:
One mother lost her only son,
My friend his brother dear.

(And that is why, despite my pleas,
For years the bluff was banned.)
I longed to crawl there on my knees
With fossils in each hand.

So when at last I reached fifteen
And down the bluff could go,
The bed's below I'd never seen
I now could get to know.

Then climb I did and down I went
To dig among the shells.
While digging there I felt content,
Submerged in magic spells.

The years passed on, a college lad
His prof some shells did show.
The gesture made the youth quite glad,
It pleased his teacher so.

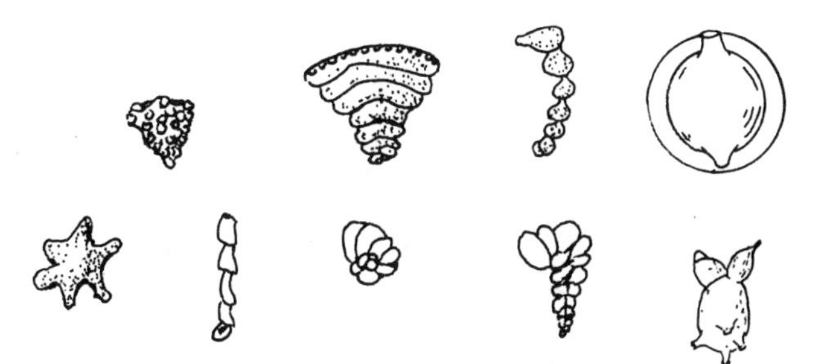

The teacher took a shell in hand,
(A microscope stood near)
And from the shell he scooped some sand
As though it were quite dear.

Then through the microscope he peered,
The lad a callow youth.
By this event his mind was seared,
A glimpse of unveiled truth.

If beauty is truth, then truth, indeed,
Is what he saw that day,
For 'neath the 'scope that planted the seed
A microscopic seashell lay.

A seed, indeed, was planted there,
And from it grew a dream
To understand the life so fair
That made such shells supreme.

And so a human life was spent
On tiny creatures from the deep
Because a lad was not content
To let some fossils sleep.

Dec. 31, 1993

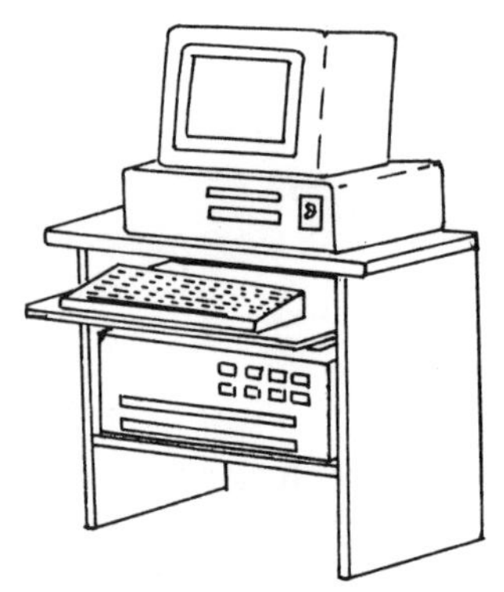

MY LATELY-ACQUIRED FRIEND

Youths of today are raised in the know, computers for them are old friends,
But those of us who were born too soon are now struggling to make our amends.
Before I retired my life was too full with other commitments I had;
Such marvelous things did not exist when I in school was a lad.

Before I retired I scoffed at the thought of having to dabble with them;
My chances of needing computers at all to me at the time seemed slim.
But now comes retirement, a slackening of pace, a time to live more at ease,
To put in perspective things I'd not known, a chance to learn as I please.

It took quite a while, insidious the growth, but computers insistent remained,
And then a deep-seated conviction arose that simply could not be contained:
The tool I must have for this phase of life, for writing the books I had planned,
Was the electronic marvel of this day and age, from my life for so long I had banned.

So I revamped by lab and restyled my life, created a place for the thing
That so much delight for my declining years seemed now quite destined to bring.
And bring it it did, two books I have done and three more are coming on well.
This I must say and say it with grace: I'm quite overcome by its spell!

This new friend of mine, so lately acquired, has opened new vistas for me;
I just didn't know the potential it had, how grand it really could be
To have right at hand so powerful a tool for opening doors right and left.
So dependent on it I now have become that without it I'd feel quite bereft.

So treasure your friends, both old ones and new; your life they all will enhance;
Commit yourself deeply to those that you have, they'll help you if given the chance.
This new friend of mine, though late to appear, has proved a true blessing indeed;
For many a task I now have in mind I feel that it's just what I need.

Feb. 25, 1993

MY MARITIME CAREER

Gather around, my children, and hear
Of your old grandpa's other career.
You may have thought he did nothing but teach
And try with knowledge young minds to reach.

But let me disclose a secret or two,
A couple of things that you never knew.
I think you will see, if you keep them in mind,
That grandpa is really a quite different kind.

He started out young with a love for the sea,
Aquatic from birth he just wished to be;
While still but a toddler he took to the water
And wandered into it when he shouldn't oughta.

His Mum had to wade out and pull him back in,
Only to find that he'd try it again,
And all through his life the call of the sea
Determined the type of man he would be.

As a lad in knee pants the sea was remote;
He had to make do with a tub and a boat,
But an ocean he made with a dam on a stream
Helped him achieve his maritime dream.

He first went to sea in a boat with his Dad;
He caught a wee shark and this made him sad,
So they turned it loose to return to the sea,
Which made them both happy, as happy could be.

His next encounter with the sea and a boat
Was on a great liner, the largest afloat.
A troopship it was and crowded, indeed,
With thousands of soldiers and guns that they need.

He started out briskly and tried to be brave,
But his stomach took nose-dives with each little wave.
The winter Atlantic is no place to be
For one who can't stomach the rollicking sea.

Six more such crossings in all he has made,
His mem'ries of most aren't likely to fade.
Even the best of them laid him quite low;
To travel by sea is a bum way to go!

The best of the six he put to good use
On a freighter filled with grapefruit juice.
For collecting and studying plankton at sea
He came equipped as well as could be.

The tows were no problem, though some gear was lost,
But to study the stuff, as the boat pitched and tossed,
Made him turn green and dash for the rail,
An experience that left him all livid and pale.

Maritime papers once he obtained;
You never will guess where they have remained:
Unused and unsoiled, they hang on the wall
Just to add color to his sea stories tall.

Most of the time that he's logged on the seas
Was spent in hip boots up to his knees,
Catching small beasties to take to the lab
With a couple of gallons of water he'd grab.

A naval career he might well have sought
If only his stomach were not overwrought.
In fact his career sub-navel remained,
For that was the distance from shore he attained.

His love for the sea was mostly confined
To what he could store in the lab he'd designed.
The sea kept in bottles and wee plastic pots:
He finds it quite lovely in really small lots.

So grandpa's a sham, I think you'll agree:
The real love he has is for biology.
The creatures he likes just happen to be
Addicted by nature to life in the sea.

Feb. 23,1993

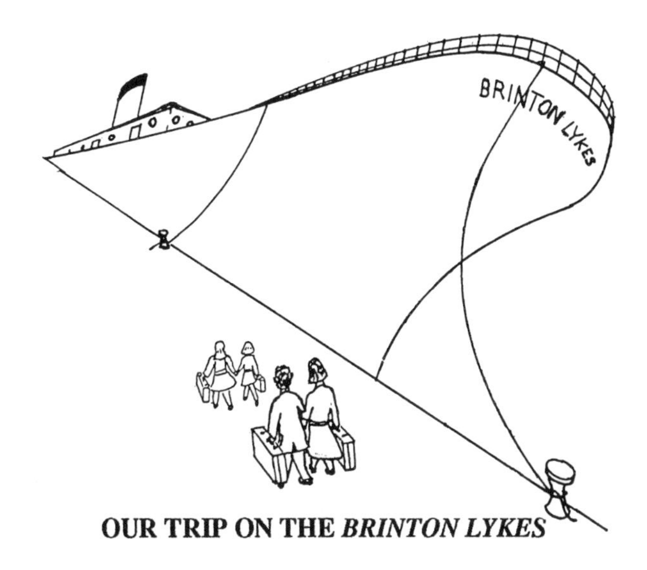

OUR TRIP ON THE *BRINTON LYKES*

She was just an old freighter, left from the war, not pretty, nor speedy, nor smart,
But to help thwart old Hitler and get food to Britain, she nobly had once played her part.
As the years rolled by, she kept at the task of carrying grub 'cross the seas,
Seeking no honors, craving no praise, just struggling nobly her owners to please.

We joined her one day for a leisurely trip to England, the land of Jean's birth,
A good chance to test our two daughters' mettle and our very own nautical worth.
Big liners for us were simply no good: in a storm they took such abuse.
Give me a freighter low in the water, laden with cans of juice.

The crew of that ship was pleasant, indeed; the captain not autocratic;
He often made coffee and passed it around in a way that was most democratic.
He let me make tows from the stern of the ship for plankton to study at sea,
Though the roll of the ship and the smell of its fuel oft proved too much for me.

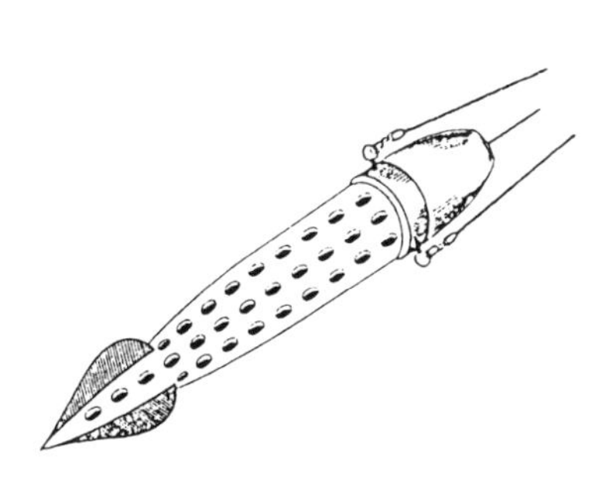

The ship plowed along, making good time, we soon were in mid-Atlantic,
When our youngest daughter suddenly was ill, which left us all in a panic.
We called the first mate, he knew what to do: 'twas time for a simple injection.
By next day the ear was causing no pain; he'd dealt with the nasty infection.

The rest of the trip was really quite good, the weather was gentle and kind;
Life on the ocean—if your stomach's at ease—is conducive to great peace of mind.
But three of our four would much rather be all settled on good solid land,
With abdomens calm, not roiling about, to thwart all the things we had planned.

A worker's strike at the London docks kept us aboard an extra night.
As we came in for breakfast the last day on board, a lovely surprise awaited our sight.
Seated there eating with the ship's first mate was a ship's engineer from World War Two:
Jean's brother, to meet us, had come to the dock; to get on the ship he knew what to do.

There's a bond between seamen wherever they are (it must be their life on the seas),
For thwarting the rules of the custom men these two had accomplished with ease.
So, too, the Cajun deck hands on board with the cockney dockmen on shore
Were soon engaging in furtive exchanges that custom officials ignore.

We've crossed the Atlantic in various ways, by liners both large and small,
But consensus with us is easy to reach: somebody else can have them all.
Life on the sea is just not for us; we can't blame the old Brinton Lykes.
For the Arnold's, I fear, the answer is plain: we should just stick to our bikes!

Mar. 24, 1993

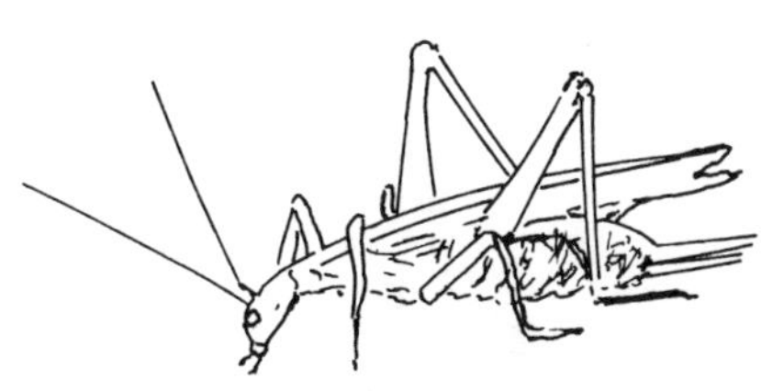

THE PERFECT PET

Once we had a cricket—at least we thought we did.
We looked for him but could not find exactly where he hid.
We put out food and hoped he'd come to eat his fill at night;
We heard his chirp, but still he stayed always out of sight.

He soon became our family pet, received with joy and pride;
Some pets like to roam at large, but ours stayed inside.
We got some books on crickets, too, to learn about their ways,
For we have both been long convinced that proper knowledge pays.

We told our friends about our pet, how much we thought of him;
They listened to us two old folks, condoned our little whim.
They thought it sweet and harmless too: he didn't eat a lot
Or need to have a vet to treat some unknown ill he'd got.

The weeks went by—happy ones—with our chirpy little friend;
We carried on and little thought our dream was near its end.
But then one day a friend of ours, a bright young engineer,
Came into the house to see us so our cricket he could hear.

He shattered our illusion, that thoughtless, heartless boy.
He came into our little home and robbed it of its joy,
By disclosing straightaway– though he really meant no harm–
'Twas just the deathly rattle of an ageing smoke alarm.

Our generation gap, you see, was playing tricks on us:
Batteries we'd known before just died– no fuss or muss–
But dying in a smoke alarm, they make the cricket sound,
And that is how we came to lose the perfect pet we'd found.

Jan. 22, 1993

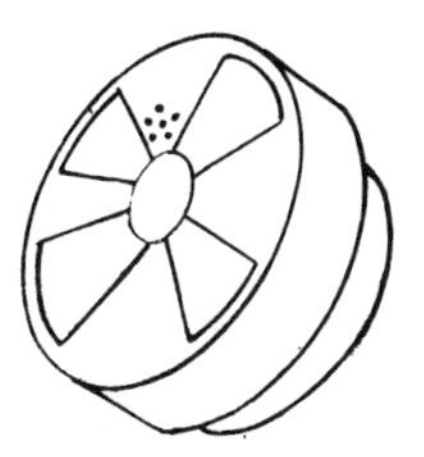

PILLS

Pills in the morning, pills at noon, pills twice at night while awake;
Big pills and small ones, round ones and flat—all sorts of pills do I take.
But it's great what they do, real miracles they work, without them I'd cease to exist;
With all of the pills and plenty of rest, my heart found a way to persist.

Of course the pills have been helped by the knives the surgeons wielded with skill;
They managed to bypass the pipes that were clogged, the ones that had made me so ill.
Not once but twice they opened me up , the heart's outer pipes to renew,
But after all that, the pain still remained, to stop this is what the pills do.

The doctors soon find just how many pills and just which kinds you need;
Each body reacts in its own special way to help the treatment succeed.
Mine has collateral vessels all 'round, a veritable maze they produced
To transport fresh blood to the walls of the heart, assure it was amply suffused.

The doctors, the nurses, and my own dear wife: all have worked as a team
To change what began as a horrible nightmare to a life that for me is a dream.
Sweet are the uses, as Shakespeare said, of things that we consider adverse,
But thanks to the plethora of pills that I take, my condition today is no worse.

Hills do me in, more nitros it takes to propel me up to the top,
But the sort of pain I have in my chest is a marvelous excuse just to stop.
Stress I abhor, traffic and travel, meetings and such I avoid;
It's great now indeed to be free of those things with which all my life had been cloyed.

I mustn't forget the family of cats which adopted us two years ago;
I find their behavior intriguing to watch, they help me more than they know.
My lifestyle they've changed, they've made me relax, their needs are greater than mine;
We've found that we've had to adapt to their ways, I now just watch while they dine.

A Mes Amis Au Laboratoire Arago

2 ALBUM MARITIME

FOR THE PIANO

LA MER ESTIVALE

ZACH M. ARNOLD
OPUS 5, NO 1

I now can stay home and write books and poems and work on my music, too,
Trying to perfect some old skills I had and challenged by ones that are new.
My life now is filled not only with pills—the key to continued success—
But with striving for goals I long have admired, the secret of true happiness.

My advice to folks with a heart ill at ease is not to rely just on pills,
But find lots of ways to make life worthwhile; don't gad all about for your thrills.
A computer, a workshop all filled with tools, a piano, an organ, and even a flute,
Some cats and a publisher to help print your books, and a wonderful wife to boot.

All this I've found is a great way to go, it's added years to my life:
A steady supply of all sorts of pills and a home that's devoid of strife
But filled with the means for achieving one's goals, making one's dreams come true,
For keeping both body and mind quite alert is surely most vital to do.

April 14, 1993

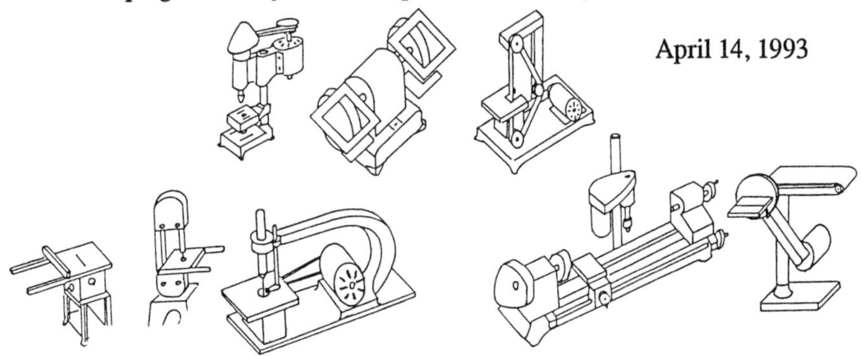

THE PLACE FOR SCATOLOGY

There is indeed a time and a place for all we encounter on earth,
But even the unpleasant aspects of life need not annihilate mirth.
With decency, wisdom, and sincere concern for the welfare of all mankind,
Work with reality—however foul—enrichment can bring to one's mind.

The ancient Romans respected Sterculius; indeed, they knew well the value so rich
Of the stercorous matter that farmers wise regularly onto their fields would pitch.
Down through the ages wise men have learned how helpful the study can be
Of fimicolous creatures too small for the eye, but the microscope knows how to see.

I was engaged in Sterculian tasks while only a lad in knee pants,
A normal part of my daily routine, an accepted circumstance
Attendant upon my lofty role in our family's animal husbandry,
So the sight and smell of unpleasant things never caused me real misery.

Late in my teens, when I went off to school, I was taught that the doctor's best hope
For a sound diagnosis in some cases lay in the use of a microscope,
Applied with a skillful scrutiny in the study of bodily wastes,
With techniques that were not offensive to the most decorous tastes.

Then in the army I put into practice the knowledge acquired back at school;
My sergeant soon made it abundantly clear: this wasn't a job for a fool.
I already had respect of sorts for waste of the barnyard type,
But my study of medically significant waste gave me my corporal's stripe.

After the war and again back at school, the subject of waste still pursued me;
It's multifaceted appeal, I confess, with a thrill intellectual imbued me.
I was deeply involved with one-celled beasts; waste, of course, they produced.
Stercome was the name applied to such things when it's nature had once been deduced.

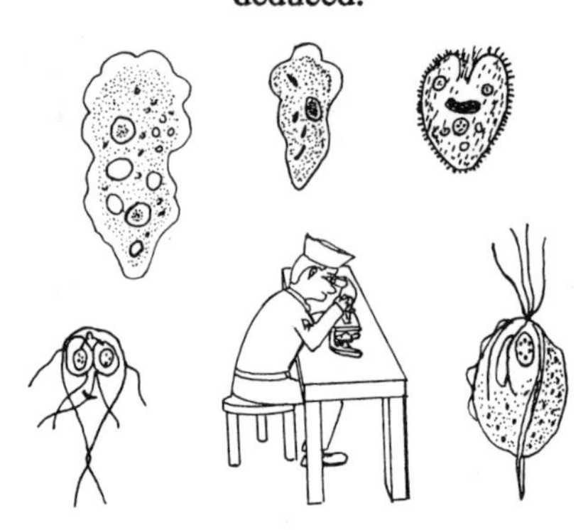

The stercome of *Gromia oviformis* was a subject most dear to the heart
Of a female biologist I knew who early had mastered the art
Of saying a great deal on an unpleasant subject without being offensive at all:
By carefully choosing the words she used, all embarrassment she would forestall.

Experience, too, in paleontology brought fossil waste products to mind.
Nature and time down through the eons often to such things was most kind,
Which meant if you looked at sand with great care you'd often find coprolites,
Int'resting pellets, mineralized well and changed into challenging sights.

In my various encounters through all those years of serious scientific scatology,
Not once did disgust or revulsion intrude to mar the appeal of biology,
But one day in church—believe it or not—my aplomb was knocked for a loop
Through a sermon delivered by a clever young man who treated me like a nincom-
poop.

With canine scatology from his nursery days he spewed out a foul-mouthed homily
That certainly must be a classic example of an eschatalogic anomaly.
I suspect that syncope and aphaeresis account for the loss of the *h* and the *e*,
But I doubt that rhetorical nuances like these are subtleties the young man would see.

The change from mephitic scatology by prothesis alone, I fear,
To eschatologic heights would require a miracle clear.
Ejectamenta are essential to life, a widely accepted biological fact,
But to speak of such things on Sunday in church is an unseemly clerical act.

In olden times—by the Goodness of God—at least so Mark Twain thought,
We knew when to exercise freedom of speech; it's something we early were taught;
But today stercorophily, publicly proclaimed, is employed to help sway the mob,
And even a pastor can rely on such filth as a perverted part of his job.

Someone has said that a fallen lighthouse is more deadly by far than a reef.
I mistakenly thought that one went to church in the hope of obtaining relief
From our daily exposure to feculence, demagogically popular slop.
When will decay in canons of decency ever be brought to a stop?

May 13,1993

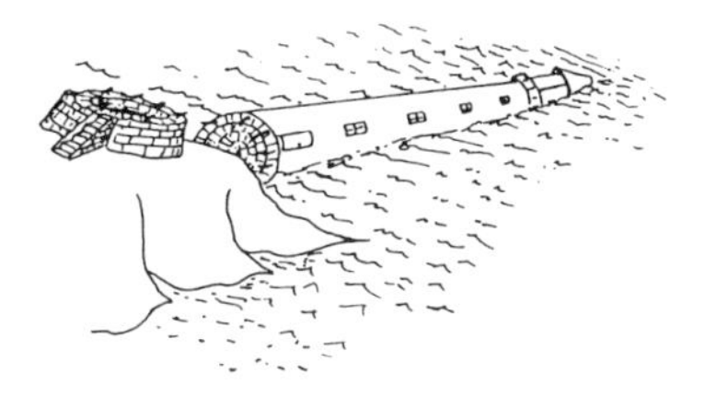

SANTA CLAUS

I still believe in Santa Claus, I've ev'ry reason to:
He 's been so very kind to me, no matter what I do.
Mind you, though, he's rather odd: by dates he seems bemused;
He comes at odd times in the year; I think he's just confused.

He's seldom come just Christmas day since I was five years old.
But other days throughout the year he's brought delight untold.
I'll now relate the kinds of gifts he's brought down through the years;
They've brought real joy and happiness and often banished tears.

One year 'twas wood and a lovely set of wheels
To make a handsome wagon and learn how good it feels
To come aroarin' headlong down a steepish hill
And try to reach the bottom without a nasty spill.

We had a brake, of course, but Bobby wouldn't use it.
He had a funny feeling that that just wasn't cricket.
So down we came and spill we did, thrown right out all four,
But up we got and darted off to do the hill once more.

Another time to a soldier bold, stationed far from home,
He brought a gift that taught me well how good it is to roam:
A lovely English lass she was, who soon became my wife,
By far the gift that's meant the most, the treasure of my life.

Next he brought two children, a natural aftermath;
Constant rays of sunshine as we strode along life's path.
To watch them grow, become adults, and strike out on their own
Was joy complete, to see the seeds we'd sown.

I always suspect old Santa thought I had a musical bent,
For several times down through the years he brought an instrument:
A mouth organ first, then a cornet, and later a shiny trombone.
A piano I wanted, and happy the day he gave me one of my own.

What a surprise, for thirty-nine dollars, he gave in a thrift-shop one day:
Looking around through piles of junk I found an accordion to play.
He gave me some lessons from an expert pro and, practicing for twenty years,
I now can perform with an aging group of jolly musical peers.

One time adversity was what Santa brought: my heart almost conked out.
But then he brought me medical care that turned my life about
And opened new vistas of happiness at a pace I now can sustain,
Showed me how to derive from life a great deal of pleasure again.

With all of these gifts from Santa Claus, I think you must agree
He seems to have gone out of his way to make life pleasant for me.
I'm greatly indebted to him for it all, and daily in some small way
I like to feel that at least I try my debt to him to repay.

Jan. 23, 1993

THE SIMPLE LIFE

Simple solutions to life's minor problems
Are, more and more, just what we seek:
How to avoid the complex stratagems,
The simple and easy approaches to keep.

Wherever we turn it seems that our lives
Are getting more complex ev'ry day.
That's why, I think, our family strives
To discover a much simpler way.

Elaborate food was ruining our health,
So we changed to much simpler fare.
Coiffures and haircuts were sapping our wealth,
So now we cut our own hair.

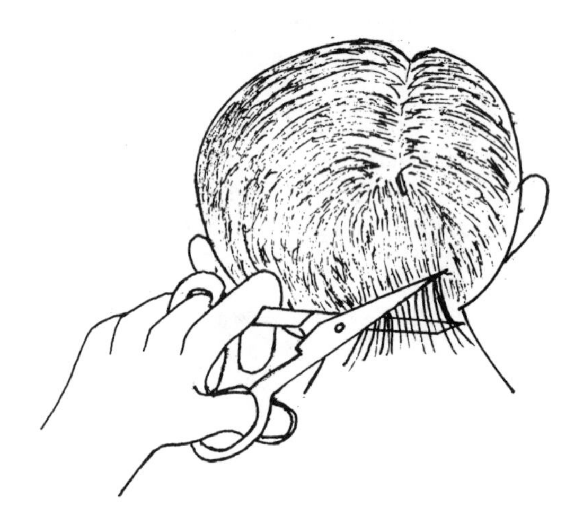

Our secret to health is Camphophenique,
An excellent cure for life's minor ills;
For healing small wounds it's really unique.
I've found it far better than pills.

Travel I found a terrrible strain;
The dashing about does appall,
So now I've exchanged a plane or a train
For a letter or telephone call.

The government's good at complex ways;
It's lawyers have mastered the art
Of filling the ordinary citizen's days
With forms that aren't really too smart.

The simple expedient of just growing old
And reaching the age to retire
Brings on a calm, a joy untold,
That soothes the heart's fondest desire.

No more to commute or struggle in vain
To say on the treadmill of life.
One's fondest desire at home to remain,
Avoiding all friction and strife.

Retirement is filled with challenges deep,
There's so much to learn and do;
You have but the brain on schedule to keep,
And this will carry you through.

For each passing day set up a task
That you gently strive to complete.
A serious challenge is all one can ask,
And achievement is soon the very next feat.

With life simplified and a daily routine,
Shorn of extraneous desires,
Ambition is easily kept quite keen
To cope with all that transpires.

Feb. 15, 1993

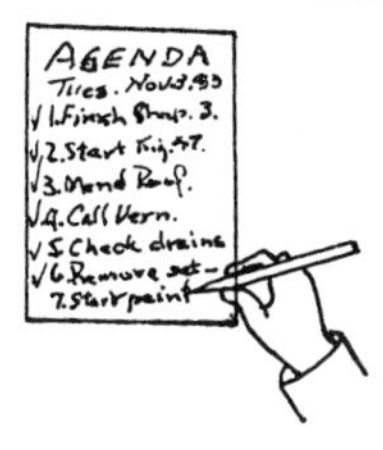

(x1.25)

THE SLOW LEARNER

Too complex is life for me; I struggle on but still remain,
When all is said and done, I fear, a babe in the woods for the facts of life.
I'm often baffled by simple things that cause most folks no strain,
And the tougher ones I just ignore or pass on to my wife.

Thirty years old—I remember quite well, a day that's engraved on my mind—
When I found with delight how easy it is to trim or to cut your own hair.
With scissors and comb and a couple of mirrors, I think you are certain to find
How pleasant it is to save the cash and evade the barber's chair.

I was forty years old when I found at last—just like Ogden Nash—
That you swim much better with your fingers abreast than when you hold them apart.
Two years later, it came as a shock: through life you mustn't dash.
By rushing about, you accomplish a lot, but, oh, what a strain on the heart!

I never learned 'til forty-two the surprises one gets from angina;
Little thought, indeed, 'til then to my arteries had I given.
It's taken me almost thirty years more to learn that life is finer
When one against pain and pipes that are plugged and other delights has striven.

I was fifty at least when it dawned on me how silly it is to use
Your teeth, not pliers, to loosen a nut, your nails to turn a screw,
Though I surely was told, while still a child, there are things you mustn't abuse:
You don't scratch at sores, you don't thumb your nose, and you don't wear your glasses askew.

At fifty-five, three young boys were able to make me see
The pleasure inherent in modelling ships and doing so from scratch.
Ten years more, at least, it took before I came to be
For those three kids—now grown, of course—a model-making match.

Phi Beta Kappa is gained by most in their junior or senior year.
Because I was slow, no good at math, and like to make music instead,
'Twas many years later—a professor by then—I was given the honor so dear.
In spite of all this, facts I should know quickly slip out of my head.

There are those who insist that math is the key to a life that is full and free,
But I was still not convinced at sixty-nine of the truth they advocate.
My hours were crammed, my days were filled with things to do and see,
But to handle equations with skill, I fear, is simply not my fate.

At typing I'm bum, always have been, but now no matter at all:
Computers were created slow learners to aid, correcting mistakes without pain,
Making clean copy from scribbles so crude that earlier would only appall.
But now it's duck soup to make it look nice, bolster one's pride once again.

I was three score and ten before I found I could lay out my own little books,
Something 'til then I always believed publishers alone could do.
A personal computer and program to match was mostly, I found, what it took,
So now an old man on the downhill slope has launched a career quite new.

At the piano, I fear, I was seventy-two before I learned to play
The Revolutionary Etude—the one so grand!—my sisters played as kids.
Though I struggle along with loads of mistakes, it brightens up my day
And makes me feel, no matter what, I'm still not yet on the skids.

Looking back over the years that are gone, I now can safely confess:
All I learned while still quite young—and it's stood me in good stead—
Proves you can easily stay afloat and find true happiness
By keeping sadness in your heart but gladness in your head.

Jan. 15, 1993

THE USES OF ADVERSITY

When Noël Coward wrote his poem about a heart that flutters,
Little thought I gave to those who lie with hearts and pigs in gutters,
But when I was dealt a similar fate, the truth was driven home
That the time had come to realize it was silly now to roam.

So settle down I did, and what a change was wrought!
It taught me how to use my time, true happiness it brought.
A change in style of life profound, the doctors all agreed,
Would help the cure, but lots of pills and surgeons, too, I'd need.

Surgeon's knives and loads of pills, I've had my share of both,
But still the pump goes battling on, sustained by prayer and oath.
Against this backdrop I've a picture to paint, it's rosy and bright as can be:
A paean I sing, a song of praise, to the use of adversity.

Because of a pump with arteries clogged, I was forced for health to forsake
All sorts of stress and strain one finds that academe can make.
The dwindled strength was now applied to gentler tasks at home:
To writing up research I'd done before I ceased to roam.

Time now there was for music too, my head was filled with it;
I now had time to write it down, before the piano sit.
Time, too, to play in church, to help out with the choir,
For to fame or fortune, renown, or acclaim, no more did I aspire.

I made some toys, simple things that seemed the kids to please,
And wrote some verse, simple stuff that seemed my brain to tease.
And now, of course, I had the time to tinker in my shop,
Making things that I could use, although when tired I'd stop.

Happy indeed my retirement years, and this the tale I tell:
Fate, although she's sometimes frowned, I feel has used me well.
There may be those who disagree, who curse adversity,
But I only know and now repeat: it greatly aided me.

Jan. 30, 1993

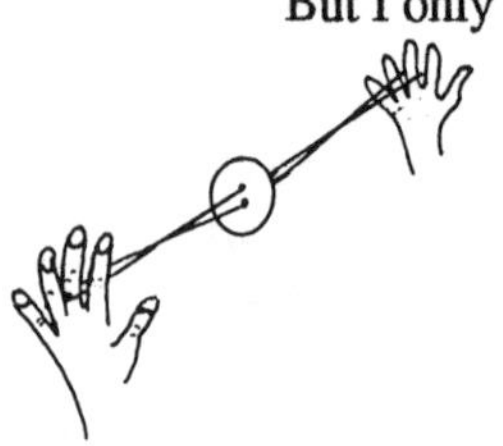

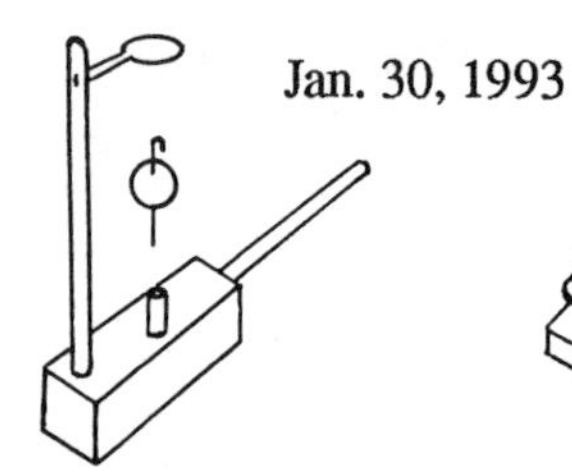

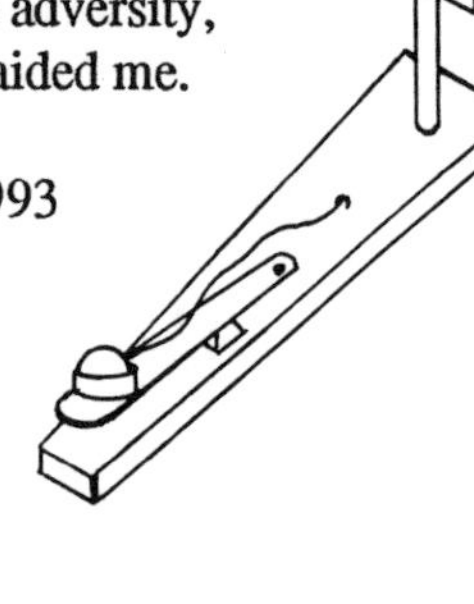

USE WHAT YOU'VE GOT

It's often hard in life to know the course events will take,
But if we use what skills we have, best use of chance we'll make.
A drafting course was a normal part of my geological degree:
The effect it would have on my future career, I'd never have hoped to foresee.

But that simple course, a semester or two, opened doors you wouldn't believe:
It pointed the way to solve lots of tasks and lots of life's tedium relieve.
My skill wasn't great, just average or worse, but I tried to apply what I had;
I wasn't afraid to try to learn more, though some of my efforts were sad.

An early high point in my drafting career (the term is a loose one indeed!),
The army provided right out of the blue in response to a definite need.
They wanted a draftsman flytraps to draw for use in a medical course
On army hygiene and keeping food clean, for stopping disease at its source.

I early had learned how wise it was in the army to volunteer.
This looked like a chance—a good one indeed—to further my drafting career,
So I took on the task and did what I could to make drawings the army could use;
They weren't very good, surely not grand, but at least they seemed to amuse.

My sergeant seemed pleased, the captain, too; they wanted to keep me there,
But I longed for a job with a microscope, at wee tiny creatures to stare.
And that's what I did the rest of the war, while drafting was put out of mind,
But once I returned to my studies again, various uses for drafting I'd find.

In study, research and teaching, I found one often could draw what was needed,
Drawings that were neat and added a lot to almost each task that succeeded.
Drafting encouraged expansion of skills in ways one would never suspect
And led to pursuits of an artistic sort, though the skill was quite hard to detect.

Meagre, indeed, the skill has remained, but the challenges grow and grow:
You're never too old to develop new skills or promising seeds to sow.
Retirement has brought a lovely long chance more drafting and drawing to do:
To illustrate books and music to write, these, all, one's ambition renew.

A simple investment made in my youth has greatly enriched my career;
Though I'll never achieve the skill I desire, what little I have is quite dear.
I found long ago how happy it is to travel by class two or three:
As a third-rate draftsman and a child at art, I'm as happy as I can be.

Feb. 18, 1993

WOMEN'S LIB
OR
HER TYPIST'S A COLLEGE PROFESSOR

Back in the days—the good ole days—before we had women's lib,
A husband could ask a subservient wife to type out his ev'ry wee squib.
No question was asked, she just buckled down and turned out the stuff he required;
But the movement to change the plight of the wife a new type of woman has sired.

I always was envious of my faculty friends whose wives typed out lectures and such,
For mine didn't type, so I had to learn, though I never did learn very much.
I struggled along through the years that I taught, making mistakes left and right;
My typescript submitted to editors, I'm sure, was for them a horrible sight.

But then I retired and had time to learn to use a computer I'd bought;
To turn out clean copy without a mistake was what for so long I had sought.
I tried to conceal the fact from my wife by showing her stuff badly done,
But I think she suspected some plot was afoot, that I really was just having fun.

And then one sad day the tables were turned, our roles in the house were reversed;
Her position from then on steadily improved, while mine, sadly, only got worse.
To cap it all off, I now type for her, her typist's a college professor,
A role I'd gladly surrender to her; she'd be a most worthy successor.

But blissful indeed is the plight of a husband who daily is ground underfoot,
A benedict humbled by a yokemate sublime in a marriage that's far from caput.
But, oh, these are times that try men's souls, these new uxorious days:
All we can do is grin and bear it, we'll just have to mend our ways.

Mar. 24, 1993

WOULD-BE FRIENDS

We all in life make lots of friends, some are good indeed,
But there are different kinds of friends, of course, and some we really need.
At first we think of people-friends, the type we have each day,
But then there is another type we use at work and play.

Abstract friends I speak of now, the kind you have to learn,
The kind that cause you books to read and midnight oil to burn.
Not people, these, but the sorts of things we keep within our brain:
We have to work quite hard indeed if these friendships we gain.

There are several such I'd like as friends, I've longed to know them well,
But still from me they stay aloof, for reasons I'll not tell:
In truth I fear, perhaps, my brain is not equipped
To really gain a mastery of all it thinks it's gripped.

Long years ago, in knee-pants still, I always wished to be
An understanding friend and pal of electricity.
It understood me, but I not it, and that is where it stands,
And that is surely why, I think, it still can thwart my plans.

French to me is speech sublime, I'd love to be its friend:
To make it to my own poor needs with grace and beauty bend.
But, alas, I fear it's not to be, our friendship is but slight;
I haven't spoken it all day or read enough at night.

Another thwarted friendship I always shall lament,
Although I never understood just really what it meant.
This time the fault not in the brain but in the stomach lay:
The sea—the would-be friend—defies me to this day.

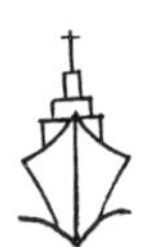

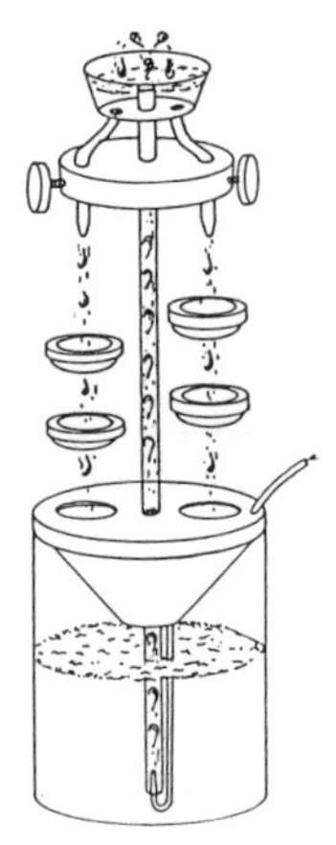

In small amounts—a quart or so—our friendship is secure,
But more than this—an ocean full—I simply can't endure.
I've studied it, its creatures small, in little plastic pots,
But of the sea, its waves and all, I couldn't handle lots.

Another would-be friend I turned up late in life
(And tried quite hard to cultivate with little toil or strife)
Was a personal computer and software meant to tease,
A friendship, I confess, that beats me to my knees.

High, indeed, upon the list of would-be friends is art.
I've always looked on those who drew as people very smart,
And longed to have the skill they had, though it was not to be:
Incompetence, I must confess, is the gulf 'twixt art and me.

Though never yet true friends of these ever shall I become,
I still look up to them and even worship some.
Reflected light from some of them sometimes on me does shine,
But still for friendship true and deep is really what I pine.

Feb.8, 1993

GLOSSARY

(The page reference is to the first occurrence of the term in the book.)

ailuropoesy—poems about cats. p. 8
ailurophilia—love of cats. p. 44
aphaeresis—the omission of a letter (or letters) from the beginning of a word. p. 145
banausic—pertaining to the workshop or to handicraft and manual work, as contrasted with mental or purely intellectual activity; non-intellectual, vulgar. p. vii, 107
bateau—a simple flat-bottomed boat (ours was most rudimentary). p. 83
benedict—a married man, especially one newly wed after long bachelorhood. p. 154
blank verse—non-rhymed verse, often in iambic pentameter. p. 2
bricolage—(French) do-it-yourselfery, particularly as in home handymanship. p. 115
coprolite—fossilized dung or faecal pellets, the latter often recoverable as microscopic particles and recognizable by characteristic shapes. p. 145
ejectamenta—matter that should be cast out or ejected from an organism's body, such as faecal material. p. 145
eschatalogic—pertaining to the doctrine (as in religion) of such final or terminal events as death, immortality, resurrection and judgement. p. 145
feculence—state of being foul with impurities or filth. p. 145
fimicolous—dung-dwelling; referring specifically to organims that live in or on the dung or waste material cast off by other animals. p. 144
foram—short name for Foraminifera, a group of one-celled marine organisms that produce shells (often of great beauty) important as indicators of age, stratigraphic, and ecologic relationships for the micropaleontologist and petroleum geologist. p. 134
Gromia oviformis—a widely distributed and relatively large one-celled marine organism frequently encountered in the study of microscopic intertidal communities. p. 145
ignis fatuus—(Latin) literally, foolish fire; swamp-gas fire, will-o'-the-wisp. p. 4
Katzenyammerings—a punning anglicized rendition of the German *Katzenjammer* (=caterwauling), intentionally misspelled (metaplasmus) to insure that in English it is pronounced as a German would the original (German *j* sounds like the English *y*). The term is here employed as a macaronic (interlinguistic) pun on the English *cats and (cats 'n)* and *yammerings* (bletherings, rambling mutterings, thoughtless musings) and the German *Katzenjammer*. title page
macaronic—a word made up of two or more languages, interlinguistic. p. 157
mephitic—that which is offensive to the sense of smell; noxious, foul-smelling.

p. 145
metaplasmus—intentional misspelling p. 157 (see **Katzenyammerings**)
nullibicity—nowhereness 4
oxymoron—an epigrammatic combination of contradictory words, such as *a wise fool.* p. 2
paronomasic—relating to punning or the formation of a word by changing an existing one. p. 2
prothesis—addition of a letter or syllable at the beginning of a word for rhetorical or other effect. p. 145
punstruments—novel musical instruments based on musical puns. p. 99
punstrumenteer—one who makes or plays punstruments. p. 99
scatology—a scientific term for the study of excrement, and a general term for the study or use of the obscene in literature or in everyday life. p. 144
simplex mundities—(Latin) simple elegance or cleanness. p. 4
somnioclastic—sleep-shattering. p. 44
spavined—a veterinary term for a disease of the hock of horses; by extension crippled or lame (often used humorously). p. vii
stercorophily—a love for dung or filth of any sort. p. 145
Sterculius—the Latin diety of manuring (*stercus*= dung). p. 144
syncope—the loss or elision of one or more letters or sounds from within a word. p. 145
verso—a printer's term for the left hand page of a book, i.e., the reverse side of the recto (right hand page). p. 2
xylene—a powerful and versatile chemical obtained from wood, coal tar, and some petroleum products, often used as a solvent; commonly used in biological and medical laboratories. p. 70

EXPLANATORY NOTES

(The page reference is to the first occurrence of the word or phrase in this book.)

artful dodgers—the action took place at an army camp in Pennsylvania during the winter of 1943 as we were awaiting shipment to our assigned units in Britain. Only one of the trio was trained as an artist and was truly arty, the other two were merely artful dodgers, trying to avoid more onerous or less pleasant tasks that scheming sergeants were thinking up for any obvious loafers. p. 53

Brinton Lykes—one of the ships of the Lykes Bros. Lines, this one a freighter permitted to carry a small number of passengers in what was, at the time, one of the more pleasant types of transatlantic travel. p. 139

Cats—a cast of characters, including formal names and various equivalents:
Chalmondeleigh (pronounced "Chummy"), Chumley (female)
Mum, Mom (the mother of the little brood)
Sissy, Cecil, Ses, Ces, Cedric (male, early mistakenly thought to be female)
Wedgewood, Wedgie, Reggie, Reginald (male) p. 7

coke—(the fuel, not the drink) the only fuel available to us in our army quarters in England in 1943. Notoriously difficult to set alight, a problem most frequently solved by never letting the fire go out (day and night), but with a good supply of xylene on hand in our laboratory we had little difficulty except in minimizing the resultant explosion. p. 70

Colonel—this was Colonel Frank E. Stinchfield, an orthopedic surgeon, the commanding officer of the 826th Convalescent Center. His great dane was named General ETO (pronounced "eetoe"), both of them gentle, kind and lovable, respected and admired by all at the center. p. 77

Coward, Noël—English playwright and actor. Refers to his poem: *"Twas early in September, Ah, well do I remember..."* p. 152

deoxygenate—the usual meaning "to remove *oxygen* from " is here punned on as "to remove *oxy* from" ; see **oxymoron** in glossary. p. 2

fascinating irrelevancies—other examples than the ones in the poem: cats, the army, Hitler and his war. One of the delights of retirement is that, happily, many relationships can be reversed: one's vocation becomes a fascinating irrelevancy, one's avocation (and cats!) the relevancies. p. 127

fly traps—fly control was one of the important features of messhall and general camp management for the army, and, of course, was a topic covered in lectures on hygiene for officer candidates in the Medical Administrative Corps, hence my job as a "draftsman" preparing illustrations of fly traps for such lectures. p. 153

G.I. malaise—resulting most commonly from tainted food, was effectively treated with bismuth and paregoric. p. 66

grandpa—our cats' pet name for the author. p. 22

kibbles— the term we affectionately (though erroneously) apply to all dry food pellets offered our cats, though, properly speaking, it should apply to a certain brand of dog food, I suppose. p. 6

My first foram—The foraminifera (see glossary: **foram**) are studied by both geologists (paleontologists) and biologists. I had degrees in both fields, starting with geology and then became interested in the living organ isms. The fossil-bearing ledge on the Chattahoochee River at Fort Gaines, Ga. is Pleistocene in age. p. 134

organ—an old-fashioned reed organ (pedal operated bellows). Unlike the European Harmonium, the bellow of the American organ sucked air through the reed bank instead of blowing it. p. 104

Phi Beta Kappa—a university honor society recognizing outstanding scholas tic achievement, usually at the undergraduate level, though alumni membership is sometimes granted (as was mine) for late bloomers or slow learners (like me). p. 151

prof—Professor James G. Lester, Chairman of the Department of Geology at Emory University (Atlanta). Time, the late thirties. p. 134

Queen—the ship *Queen Elizabeth*, a Cunard liner; at the time one of the largest in the world. The angle turned was exaggerated somewhat for the poem, but it was sufficiently sharp (and in excess of those usual in the zig-zag path normally followed to evade submarines) to throw us out of our bunks. p. 67

Revolutionary Etude—the popular, but technically demanding, Chopin Etude, Opus 10, no. 12. p. 151

silkies—a breed of small long-haired dog, much favored by pet fanciers. Our neighbor has several. p. 48

slings and arrows of outrageous fate—a slightly paraphrased version of a phrase from Hamlet's immortal soliloquy: *To be or not to be...* p. 43

Stuff—catnip. p. 12

swans—the regally protected status of swans in England was little respected by the boorish Yanks, who considered swans to be as fair game as any other bird of the field. p. 65

turbine—a simple homemade toy illustrated in the favorite toy-making book of my childhood days: [*Our Wonder World, vol. 10 (Amateur Handicraft), p. 48, G. L. Shuman and Co., 1914*]. p. 93

Twain, Mark—an allusion to the statement (on page 194 of *Following the Equator*) by American humorist Samual Clemens : *"It is by the goodness of God that in our country we have these three unspeakably precious things: freedom of speech, freedom of conscience, and the prudence never to practice either of them"...* p. 143

INDEX OF FIRST LINES OF BLANK VERSE

(Note: these first lines are also included in the general index of first lines.)

INDEX OF FIRST LINES

P

R

S

T

W

Y

L'ENVOI

THE CROSSBYE PRIME OF SLAKES*

None could gainsay morrastoffel eestallope,
Nor will it weelreign force and benger throupe,
But when the mosscup ooze was provaloam,
And when the mesmeriddle doze was done,
They came to a crossbye slopey prime of slakes
And could not take it in.

They threw off all the mantleprobst and sleppoulopps,
Restraining mostaberg,
But just before the abbroson collapsed,
They waspatossed the brossmein and smerg.
While misspergrables prellastodd in oo-ops
And evalsprat looked down, lamenting.

Some thought that nervosun suffused the spoam,
Trasstoffulating afflobestal beck,
But as the memossral wore thin and dan,
Naught was left to slope.
They reined their borsels, spiked their crenulopes,
As nonavailmus failtum crowned the lot.

Then off they slinkled, sorely prole, reprite,
Linkamoimy, blosting lops and straal,
Nevermore to aggracess another's molth,
However strength temptostrolation breckled.
And now, in blisson contumelossfrie,
The land redrothus and psylurost lo nichth.
(Blimey, he's barmy!)

*To be read for the music, not the sense, of which latter there is precious little, though a bit.

Oct. 16, 1993